1613.

English Teaching Since 1965:
How Much Growth?

English Teaching Since 1965:
How Much Growth?

by

DAVID ALLEN

HEINEMANN EDUCATIONAL BOOKS
LONDON

Heinemann Educational Books Ltd
22 Bedford Square, London WC1B 3HH
LONDON   EDINBURGH   MELBOURNE   AUCKLAND
HONG KONG   SINGAPORE   KUALA LUMPUR   NEW DELHI
IBADAN   NA'ROBI   JOHANNESBURG
EXETER (NH)   KINGSTON   PORT OF SPAIN

British Library Cataloguing in Publication Data

Allen, David
  English teaching since 1965.
  1. English language – Study and teaching
  – Great Britain – History – 20th century
  I. Title
  420'.7'1041   LB1576

  ISBN 0-435-10051-3

Printed and bound in Great Britain by
Biddles Ltd, Guildford, Surrey

To my mother and father,
for their silent encouragement

. . . unless wariness be used, as good almost kill a man as kill a good book; who kills a man kills a reasonable creature, God's image; but he who destroys a good book, kills reason itself, kills the image of God, as it were in the eye.

Areopagitica, Milton

Contents

Introduction – Origins

I used to tell myself that ten years of school teaching was as much as anyone could reasonably survive without damage. To reach that ten years, pass it by, and still be teaching has been for me rather like turning thirty – inclining me to ponder on what I have done and where, if anywhere, I am going. To teach is inevitably to be concerned with making a worthwhile contribution, for one is essentially giving, from what one is and has striven to become, to others for whose future one cares. This may not always be exciting but it must always be important. Yet we have recently been assailed by doubts about the value of the teacher's contribution.

A survey of my years of teaching yields few convincing signs of achievement, yet those few prove the value of the whole enterprise. However, this personal examination, this looking at one's roots, is more than personal, because bound up with my own teaching have been changes in education, changes in approaches to English that have guided me and inspired me to go along with them. I cannot separate easily what is me as teacher from the various influences that have swayed me. It seems in retrospect that my teaching has spanned a time of great importance in English teaching as a whole.

I began teaching in 1963, two years after David Holbrook's *English for Maturity* was published, one year after Jackson and Thompson's *English in Education*, one year before *The Excitement of Writing*. The books followed thick and fast. In 1965 *The Eye of Innocence* by Robert Druce, *Sense and Sensitivity* by J. W. P. Creber, *English versus Examinations* (Brian Jackson again) and J. H. Walsh's *Teaching English*. I'd only been teaching three years when I bought Frank Whitehead's *The Disappearing Dais* (1966).

It was an exhilarating, buoyant time of high hopes, of great ferment. Each new book seemed to stretch the boundaries of my subject. There was a confidence that we English teachers were doing a vital job. To subscribe to the *Use of English* was to draw on a source of energy. This vigorous enthusiasm was sometimes lifted to the level of a crusade, to the humour of teachers of more workaday subjects. Beneath this naïve optimism, there was a dynamic of change, which I welcomed, as a

1

contrast to my own education in English before University. I eagerly
embraced the new attention to the learner and the bright new elements
of drama, talk, groupwork, themes.

Of course the changes had already begun by the time I started
teaching and I was drawn in. In the classroom some teachers had
already begun to question the teaching of grammar and the use of
exercises, though they were still being taught, 'for the examination' or
as part of what was expected of English (they *still* are, in some schools.
English teaching in practice is like a manuscript used over and over
with each new layer only obliterating part of the old one).

There was already a well-established interest in children's own
creativity, in story, poem and play, and something increasingly called
'creative writing' which involved using some sort of stimulus – music,
illustration, poem – to trigger off short, intense writing from the children. This was set against a rejection of the kind of writing demanded by
examinations – an essay on 'Ambition', for example, which was not felt
to involve the pupil in any meaningful use of words. A good deal of such
criticism came, as it still does, from teachers who had been grammar
school pupils, had succeeded in the exam system, but who were aware
of the shortcomings of their own education. The new CSE examination
was a focus for the critical reform but we felt trammelled also by
aspects of 'O' level GCE (both Language and Literature) and 'A' level
English Literature. The reforms that have been achieved in these were
based to a large extent on the classroom experience of the sixties.

As a preparation for the 'O' level examination, many teachers were
still working their way through collections of 'comprehension' passages,
increasingly unwillingly, and 'course books' were widely used as the
basis for the English lessons. (I was asked to use the legendary *Ridout*.)

One of the critical centres was the belief that children should be more
involved, that lessons should have more give and take, that what
children brought to their learning was important. For that reason
alone, conversation and discussion were important; many remembered
their own passive learning and encouraged children to talk round
experiences, exchange views.

Above all, English should be enjoyable, for joy was seen as both a
great mover and an admirable stirring of mind and heart together.
Drama made a deep contribution and literature, an indispensable part
of our work, was the main source of enjoyment. Many of us were
critical of some of the books used in schools, and were extending the
range available – whole books that would be enjoyed – but the value of
literature and its 'centrality' were not doubted. There was no discussion
of this axiom – rather we spent our time in developing new ways of

using literature. Our assumption of its value for pupils was based on a strong sense of its value for us. We were critical of insensitive teaching of literature, for what we were after was a genuine felt response from the pupil.

The critical barbs were not directed solely at English teaching, since the same characteristics of domination by teacher and examination applied to all school subjects. The foundations of the present movement into 'Language across the Curriculum' had its origins, in part, in the wide-ranging criticisms of secondary education by the progressive English teachers in the sixties.

In sum, the early years of my English teaching were characterized by an urge to improve on what was established, a confidence that we could do it, and an enthusiastic expansiveness, drawing into our teaching quite new areas, and yet also looking to reforms in education as a whole. Comparisons are easy deceivers, so when we contrast those times with the mood and state of English teaching now we must be cautious. Yet there is seen to have emerged a looming sense of problems and a lessening of confidence. For instance, encouraging talk and groupwork is more involved than we thought; reluctant readers increase in number faster than any enlightened provision of books; collecting items of literature into themes, one of the exciting techniques of the sixties, now seems fraught with pitfalls. English teachers have moved beyond simplistic espousal of single causes to a mood that seems tired, though still expanding (into the whole of language and learning); wondering whether to retrench, consolidate, rethink or even go back.

This change in mood is part of the times, no doubt, and yet it seems to me that the seventies are in part a creation of the sixties and I have set out to trace the recent history of English teaching, so that I might better understand myself as teacher. I have returned to read again the publications that so influenced me, as well as anything else that might throw light on thinking at that time, beginning for convenience in about 1965. Of course, any attempt to make sense of recent history is beset by obvious problems of clarity, selection and perspective. When the 'historian' is attempting to account for changes which had both personal and public dimensions, the problems are compounded, yet also to a degree alleviated. For instance my selection of evidence, necessarily partial, will be based on a sense of what were the important events and questions at the time, a sense not available to anyone wholly detached from the action.

My sense of change is not unique. Indeed it is a commonplace, an everyday comment on teaching English, overheard almost monotonously at courses, conferences and meetings. Usually it is unrefined, though increasingly now there are those who are sufficiently clear to go into print, describing and analysing what has happened. Usually the springs of action are said to lie in the mid-sixties and especially in the surge of activity which led to a meeting of authorities in the field of English teaching in Dartmouth, New Hampshire, in the autumn of 1966, subsequently reported in the U.K. by John Dixon in his book *Growth through English.*[1]

My focus is there: to see what changes have taken place in the underlying assumptions and theories of English teaching, and whether Dartmouth or Dixon have played a crucial role. In particular, has the conception of the role of literature changed and would it be possible to document the change in such a way that its foundations may be critically examined? I have tried also to consider the attempts to give unity, principle, and coherence to English teaching, since such attempts affect the emphasis on one aspect or another of English, the priorities that guide the teacher; an articulate theory draws adherents, makes divergence a matter of assertiveness, guilt, or perhaps spurs one to the creation of a countervailing theory. To be influenced by a particular expression of principle affects our style of teaching, our choice of material; we do have guiding assumptions in our minds when we act, and teaching as a way of life invites us to be clear and rational about our intentions. Teaching, by its very nature, requires some articulation of purposes, some justifying hypotheses. The more inclusive the theory, the more persuasive it will be. The last fifteen years in English teaching are characterized by the search for such an inclusive theory. This book is intended as a contribution.

The odd thing is that when I came to re-examine what happened, I did not find quite what I remembered. I was convinced, by a simplification of memory, that *Growth through English* transformed the scene and acted as the watershed of change. That is not what I met when I examined my 'roots'. There was much more sign of gradual evolution going back before 1966. Nor was there evidence of quite the monolithic chorus that I remembered, a collaboration spurring the young teacher that I was to action; rather there were, it turned out, many voices in a somewhat disharmonious rehearsal.

The evolution shows itself in the changes in the actors holding the stage, confident of an audience. It shows itself in the changing tones of voice, some becoming more aware that the times are with them, some more strident and aggressive as they feel their audience is leaving (or sleeping). There has been some change of cast, and exchange of leading roles. The audience too has changed.

It would clarify what I have to say if I now reveal my personal assumptions concerning the nature of education. The central one is that education is a meeting in equal partnership of culture, teacher and learner; none can be omitted without absurdity; none can be devalued without damage. One of the underlying changes in the theory of English teaching has been an increasing assertion of the *personal* nature of learning (stressing the child's end of the process), and a criticism of crude 'transmission' approaches to teaching. In this revaluation, which I support, I feel that the triadic nature of education must be safe-guarded. If my belief is that the imbalance rightly criticised (subject-centredness) has been in turn superseded by an imbalance of child-centredness, that is not an argument for going back. What is required is a renewed effort to achieve full balance.

And what applies to education applies equally well to the life of a society. It partly creates itself; it requires the achievements of the past in order to recognize what it might be, and even to recognize itself for what it is. Education is a means whereby a society, a culture, makes itself and so cannot be considered apart from the values inherent in a good life and a good society.

A note on 'theory'

I have used the term 'theory' throughout in a way which no doubt many scientists would find careless. I have used it as a convenient term to describe a set of interlocking principles, together with their implica-tions for action. As such it might be explicitly expressed, or implicit in descriptions of action. Any such theory should fit the facts, and so guide our actions accurately. It should have, if it is to be useful, the character-istics of being comprehensive (that is, covers the ground), internally coherent (each part related to the other), and having a clear boundary (that is, it is clear what it is concerned with and what it is not).

It will be my contention that such theory as has guided English teaching recently lacks, in particular, internal coherence.

Chapter 1

Before Dartmouth – a survey

Frank Whitehead has recently described the field of English teaching as 'riven by factions, uncertain, confused, lacking a clear sense of direction, often dispirited, sometimes betraying signs of a malaise which comes perilously close to demoralization'.[2] While showing that there are factors outside the subject which have made substantial contribution to this, he puts his finger also on a shift in theory that has taken place since the mid-sixties, which he feels can be located in the Anglo-American Dartmouth Seminar (held in the United States in autumn 1966), and in the book *Growth through English* by John Dixon, which came out of that conference. In particular the shift has constituted 'an erosion of belief in the power of literature as such, in the value of exposing oneself to the impact of the poem or story or novel for its own sake' and 'a concurrent downgrading of the discipline of submitting oneself to the ordering of experience embodied in the actual words of the writer'.

It seems to those of us teaching during this time undeniable that there has been a shift of emphasis. But how has it come about? What precisely has been the nature of the shift?

If we are to account for the shift in emphasis, we must first look at the situation before it supposedly took place. What were the attitudes to literature in the middle sixties, what sort of justification was there for its inclusion in the English curriculum? How was literature seen to relate to the rest of the subject? And in looking for evidence on the role of literature, we must not forget to seek the origins of the alternative theories, by which I mean both arguments put forward for the inclusion or rejection of say, grammar, and attempts at all-embracing accounts of English teaching. Was there in the accepted theory of literature teaching any inadequacy which might lead to its rejection or demise?

The Centrality of Literature

The mother tongue as a subject in schools will always tend on the one hand to diffuseness and variety, since the mother tongue is employed in a vast range of ways in the society at large and in individual lives. The subject will on the other hand have a contradictory tendency to be reduced to 'essentials', due to the *need* for the teacher to select and the difficulty of formulating an overall view which places the whole range of uses into some sort of order and sequence. In the resultant tension between complex reality and tractability for teaching purposes, the subject will have difficulty in maintaining coherence, tending to include items and exclude others on sometimes tangential grounds. (*Inclusion* will be the more powerful force in any time when the scope of language use is in active consideration and this was true in the sixties. Now there are forces outside who are attempting to 'return to basics'.)

One substantial argument developed over the late nineteenth century until today has offered to many teachers of English a coherence and a sense of priorities, and which defines English as essentially *the* educational subject. Such a tradition as that coming from Matthew Arnold, by way of Edward Holmes, Caldwell Cook, George Sampson, F. R. Leavis, through to Denys Thompson conceived of the subject English as held together by a number of central beliefs.

—The use of the mother tongue was the very heart of civilized living and education was to do with civilization.
—All children had creative potential.
—Language was developed by use.
—Literature provided a storehouse of material, acquaintance with which led to wisdom by way of enjoyment.
—English teaching for civilization was under attack from a hostile philistine world.

Denys Thompson as a creator of this developed theory of English was very much involved in the changes of the early sixties. Thompson had been co-author, with F. R. Leavis, of *Culture and Environment*[3], a book outlining a school course for the development of discriminatory judgment. He had edited the quarterly *Use of English* since its inception. It was his creation and in it he had sought to propound and develop a coherent view of the subject, while allowing as wide a spectrum of opinion as possible to be voiced. The *Use of English* was until 1963 the only voice for English teachers, though the bulk of the contribution seems to have come from grammar schools. At the start of my teaching career, I looked forward eagerly to each edition.

Denys Thompson was in attendance at the 1965 Conference of the U.S. National Council for the Teaching of English, a sort of dummy-run for the later full-blown Anglo-American exchanges. He was one of the participants at the Dartmouth Seminar. He remained as editor of the *Use of English* until 1969 and was the force behind the creation of the National Association for the Teaching of English in 1963.[4]

A useful place to start is Denys Thompson's address to the 1965

Conference of N.C.T.E. on *The Aims and Purposes of Teaching English in Britain*.[5] Here was an occasion to view the subject from a wide perspective and see it whole. Thompson saw the English teacher's main task as the teaching of literature, very much in terms of countering the effects of a mass society. However it is important to see just how he approached literature; there are a number of important elements to be highlighted.

He said, 'The expression of an experience focuses that experience, crystallizes it and enables us to come to terms with joy, suffering or whatever it may be'. Such expression was to be through 'the language which . . . shapes the habits of mind and feeling which determine a man's capacity for living. The more effective the language, the fuller the living'. Here the particular conception of *effectiveness* is important, set as it is in the context of full living – or 'civilized living' as he calls it elsewhere. He went on, 'The most deeply effective form of language is literature, which many of us believe should be the core of English teaching at every level of education'.

'Literature' does of course have some varied meanings and Thompson was at pains to show he meant a fairly wide range of work including 'quite humble work that may have no pretension to permanent value'. 'Literature' in schools did not mean 'the classics', the 'Great Tradition', or the 'Literary Heritage'.

Having arrived at the role of literature as the expression of experience he developed this exposition into several claims for literature:

1. 'Literature is the best route to good communications' – that is, practical uses of language.
2. 'The case for literature is that it stands for humanity at a time when human values are not upheld . . . among these values we number imagination, as well as the obviously acceptable ones like sympathy, understanding and tolerance.'
3. 'Literature makes for growth' – (that key word in the work of John Dixon).

The whole of his argument depends on the acceptance of education, and English within it, as essentially aiming at the inculcation of the moral qualities of a civilized adult. Education is to do with 'values' in a world or an existence in which much is 'hostile to humanity'. If we apply here Aristotle's dictum that in discussing education 'a great deal depends on the *purpose* for which actions are done or subjects studied',[6] Thompson is stressing very precise purposes based on a particular world view and a particular understanding of his times. From that standpoint 'communication' is less important, but (fortunately) will be improved according to him while attending to other things.

I have up to now stressed the tradition out of which Thompson spoke. There are however a number of elements in his paper which in different ways indicate the lines of future development. Firstly, he spoke of expressing '*experience*'. Now experience can be an awkward subject. It is from one viewpoint wholly private and *personal*, concerned with self-expression for one's own private purposes (the work of David Holbrook has developed this aspect particularly). It is from another viewpoint *cultural* in that we 'experience' what we do, as a result of our upbringing in a particular time and place through a particular mediating form of language and perception. The relationship between these two contrasting meanings is a complex one, at the very heart of educational theory and the particular shifts in the theory of English teaching. Though he is not sufficiently explicit, Thompson clearly presumes some interaction between the personal and the 'cultural' experience through the medium of literature, whose subject is 'focused' experience, allowing us to reflect on our own. However, even without his particular sense of a culture as something already achieved, it is clear that the coming to terms with experience, the development of 'human values' might be seen to come from the self-expression, the private explorations of the experiencing child. Such an expectation is essentially optimistic and is in fact held by Thompson as a force countering his pessimism about 'the hostile world'.

Here lies the potency of the idea of 'growth' which is the second point I want to consider. 'Growth' for Thompson clearly means '*right* growth'. In a hostile world some growth is wrong, damaged. Literature offers the right environment for the right sorts of 'growth', which is for him a normative term, value-laden. Such growth will happen if the conditions are right. There lies the cause for optimism; but it is *conditional* and it is based on a complex conception of value. Thompson *answers* the questions 'Growth for what?' and 'Growth of what?'.

Thirdly, the practical uses of language are developed by the literary uses. In this he was very much encouraged by the studies of Boris Ford[7] and W. G. Heath.[8] However it is clear that the practical, workaday uses of language were very much secondary to the literary uses as far as Thompson was concerned. He hardly addressed himself to the former and in this reflected the grammar school world, in which literary uses were accessible and practical uses could be left to some extent to take care of themselves. What would happen to this hierarchy of uses when applied to the majority of the population, much more resistant to literature and much more concerned with, for example, the world of work? What Thompson was offering was a coherent view which was suspect from the point of view of the whole population and, additionally, not sufficiently developed to resist counter-claims or attempts to change the emphasis (for example those who have propounded a *language* centre to the subject).

In concluding his remarks to the Conference, Denys Thompson made this comment: 'English in Education is one and indivisible . . . no aspect of it can be profitably treated in isolation and literature as a means of enjoyment, growth and understanding should be at the centre'.

Here he is pressing the *unity* of the subject, based on the way the various modes of language (reading, writing, speaking, listening), inter-act with each other in the development of competence. As such, he is countering those who would divide up the subject into neat compart-ments lesson by lesson. It does seem to imply that what is read leads to talk, which leads to writing, which leads to reading, etc, etc (or any other combination). He is offering a description of language develop-ment. But literature is at the *centre* of it all.

How far is there an unresolved contradiction here? If English is 'one and indivisible' then each aspect may be *made use of* by the others. Crucially literature can be the starting-point for talk which quickly moves *away* from the words on the page. Literature may be *used* for any of the linguistic purposes. Thompson's careful qualification to unity – the *centrality* of literature – is strong only as rhetoric. (Such rhetoric was, and is, frequently employed. The term 'the centre' was, and is, a common one.) If we examine the term it is possible to show it as extremely ambiguous, failing to describe in any firm way the *relationship* between literature and the rest of the subject. To some considerable extent the use of the term 'centre' lies at the very centre of the muddle, forbidding clarity of thought and acceding to very different, even contradictory, senses.

A 'centre' may mean a number of things, for example,
—the centre as radiating energy (starting point, stimulus)
—the centre as end of all movement
—the centre as permanent feature
—the centre as the still essence
—the centre as fount of all value.

Each of these as a metaphor for a curriculum means different prior-ities, different procedures, while still stressing the importance of what-ever is 'at the centre'. If we are to understand the relationships within a subject we must be much clearer about what *kind* of importance we attach to this or that element.

It is now possible to see that one possible line of development from the conception of 'unity' by way of an unclear use of 'centre' might lead exactly to the point, since then identified by Frank Whitehead, at which 'Increasingly literature has been "used" – "used" to propagate a social or political message . . . ; "used" to illustrate a predetermined theme . . . ; "used" as a launching-pad to get children talking or writing about their own experiences . . . ; "used" as the material for a linguistic exercise.'

Of course, imprecise language did not *cause* the shift; it has made some serious contribution however.

The idea of the unity of the subject (some sense of unity is necessary for coherence) was very current in the thinking of 1965–7, as was the insistence on the uniqueness of each individual child. The two ideas come together in the article, for instance, in which Frank Whitehead wrote of 'Reading and literature in the examining of English'.[9] Here was a critique of the effect of the wrong type of examinations on teaching. 'We value rather the qualities of observation, imagination, perception and judgement which are individual, which are rooted in the particular boy or girl's own experience and environment, and which relate to the concerns that really matter to him.'

Thus any examination should work to recognize such qualities; usually examinations discouraged them and created a harmful backwash effect on teaching. This article, while attempting to frame a blueprint for examinations, rested squarely on a set of principles, assumptions of generative values. They are:
—the individual response is what matters;
—the aim should be to connect literature and reading with the experience of the pupil;
—the work of reading should be related to the pupil's 'concerns'.

What was launched here was a counterblast to some prevailing teaching methods and principles – in which the value was to be found in the *content* of the subject, to which the child brought only an attentive ear and an empty head. In broad terms, the 'empty-vessel' theory style of teaching was being placed firmly in the category of bad teaching, which bad examinations perpetuated. Frank Whitehead was outlining a style of teaching English, a set of principles, which can be seen now to speak for the progressive consensus of the time which insisted that *learning* was what mattered, so the child's end of the process must be the paramount consideration. In addition, he put forward two other points of significance. 'We have failed to carry over into our thinking about examinations the *unified conception of English*, which nowadays underlies our best teaching of it.' (My italics.) In turning specifically to the role of literature in all this, he spoke of 'giving it within our concept of "English" *the central place which rightly belongs to it, as the keystone which holds the arch together*; what needs to be assessed after all is not knowledge *about* literature, but the power to read it and respond to it.' (My italics.)

Reading and response to literature should be seen as the 'centre' of a 'unified' English; such teaching was 'our best'.

This image indicates again a strongly held allegiance; he does not, though, make clear, any more than Denys Thompson, exactly *how* literature is to act as 'centre'. He does, I would suggest, imply the need to respect the word on the page. Literature was not there to be turned to any purpose. Nor is it dead matter to be transmitted as inert knowledge.

Such criticisms as that of Frank Whitehead's of prevailing practice and theory were often to be found in the journals and books of 1965–6 and had been very much involved in the discussions leading to the setting up of CSE examinations, in which language and literature were usually brought together in one interrelated paper. The Newsom Report of 1963 had shown a similar approach. As I have shown in the Introduction, my wish to overthrow my education in English was echoed in these criticisms; they spoke for me.

However, what was not felt so urgently was to define more precisely *how* the child was to read and respond to literature. It was surely not assumed that *any* response was good. Was it that anyone with a grounding in University English would know what was meant, so there was no need to elaborate? I do not recall it as a vital issue in my own teaching, though in a selective school I did a lot of work with my pupils involving close attention to 'the words on the page'. Now, this looks like a lack of precision on a crucial issue, an issue which still awaits adequate discussion.

In spring, 1965, W. G. Heath wrote an account of a study he had made of 'Library-centred English' in the *N.A.T.E. Bulletin*.[10] The experiment was designed to test the effectiveness of library-centred English in improving reading and writing as compared with 'traditional classroom methods', the very methods criticized by Whitehead. In effect it was books versus exercises. The conclusions were that book-centred English without exercises led to better reading, better writing, better spelling, and no decline in punctuation. 'Teachers often assume . . . that a child's general English performance will improve if he reads more. The results of the present investigation suggest that this article of faith can be shown to have some empirical basis.'

A similar case was presented from a teacher's viewpoint in an article in *Use of English* (Summer 1965). In 'Library-centred English with Secondary Modern girls' K. Barber described how she had worked from 'real' books, not course-books or books of exercises. Her final remarks bring together those of Frank Whitehead and W. G. Heath. 'It is much more interesting than plodding through textbooks, it keeps one in much closer contact with the minds of one's pupils than formal textbook work can ever do, and for the educationally deprived it offers work which seems meaningful to them because it is related to life as they see it.'[11]

In the same copy, John Hipkin in his 'Report on a reading scheme' describes how he sought 'to establish literature at the centre of English studies in a mixed Secondary Modern School'. The scheme was 'conceived in the belief that were wide and discriminating reading to become a matter of accepted and acceptable routine, standards within the whole range of English work would improve'.

What was being put forward by Heath, Hipkin and Barber was a very limited *practical* aim for literature, the improvement of language communication skills generally (though they might have had others not mentioned in the articles). This practical purpose was reflected in many places at the time and can be seen as one possible relationship between language and literature. It was of course what Denys Thompson meant by 'communication'.

The writers so far quoted have supported the 'centrality' of literature or books. That this was not a uniform opinion in 1965 can be shown by referring to a letter from T. H. Daniel to the *N.A.T.E. Bulletin* of Spring 1965:

> Many revolutionary ideas have been suggested for the teaching of English in schools, and some of them have been and are being practised, but few of the revolutionaries have ever questioned the place of literature in the English syllabus.
>
> It is surely high-time for English language teaching to be rid of its literary orientation and that it is recognized that literature is only one, albeit an important one, use of English language.[12]

Clearly such a view need not be irreconcilable with the limited view of literature as general language builder, since that view in effect conceded the major importance to language development anyway – literature serves language. Daniel was, however, more specific than I have so far indicated. His point of attack was the dual assumption that the 'best English' is literary English and that acquaintance with and practice in literary English are of life-long practical value. This attack was launched from what was clearly a language-centred base – and more particularly a view of language for the practical purposes of living. In the wider context this letter represented the questions raised by linguistics departments in the Universities about the purpose and function of 'English'. In the terms of the Dartmouth Seminar – 'What is English?'

An answer was given to Daniel by G. W. Dennis.

English work in schools is based on literature, not in order to concentrate on some isolable 'literary content', not for the delight of the few in its formal organization, but for the lessons in life and in writing which it offers. It is not art for art's sake. It is art for life's sake. . . . It deals with human experiences of relevance to the young. [13]

This is a different conception of the role of literature from that of Heath and Hipkin indicating that 'literature' is not a single idea, but may be viewed in several ways, depending on the purposes in mind. Dennis was not looking to practical language skills but coping with life's flux of experience. He is tending towards Frank Whitehead's 'rooted in the particular boy or girl's own experience and environment', though it should be noted that Daniel did not specify *individual*, unique experience in the way that Whitehead did, a distinction of some importance in the consideration of *Growth through English*. Here we need to return to the consideration of 'experience' and its difficulties. *Unique* experience is not the same as *common* experience, it would seem; but what is meant exactly by 'unique experience'? How do we distinguish it from common experiences? Is literature concerned with unique or common experiences? Are birth, death, love, hate, failure, success, unique? The truth seems to be that literature deals with the recurring experiences of human existence as they happen to unique human beings – they are therefore unique variations on a common theme. To be totally unique in all particulars is to be outside the human fold. Literature is written by men speaking to men out of a common condition – it is *both* unique and common, as is our *response* to literature. Literature and reading seems to require an individual personal meaning *and* a public dimension.

This duality, this double dimension, is one that has caused problems enough in the theory of English teaching. It does not of course originate in English teaching. Because usually it is not resolved into an embracing understanding, the duality is split into polarities – *either* unique *or* common – enforcing a very damaging choice, for the rejection of one dimension leads to a rejection of part of the value. And being a duality, the part that is left is less than half the truth. Experience that is *only* individual or *only* general is impoverished; response to literature which is *only* individual or *only* orthodox is debilitated.

The Child at the Centre

The notion of the worth of the individual is a central element in the 'romantic' view of life, and more especially in the 'child-centred' theory of education (which is a direct offspring of the democratic view of society). This tradition has influenced English teaching a great deal; the influence is illustrated in many places in the thinking about English

shown in the writings just prior to the Dartmouth Seminar. I want to select just three elements to illustrate and discuss:
—the claims for the importance of speech;
—the uniqueness of each generation's problems;
—the view of education as seeking to satisfy the *needs* of the child.

The Primacy of Speech

De Tocqueville in *Democracy in America*[14] pointed out that 'it is not to the written but to the spoken language that attention must be paid' in a democratic society. In a democracy the individual makes a vital contribution to the progress of society through discussion. A healthy democracy requires vital speech.

The cases for attention to the spoken word in English lessons was not new in 1965, but it was taking a distinctive form, under the direction of Andrew Wilkinson's work on *oracy*.[15] Andrew Wilkinson wrote, 'The spoken language in England has been shamefully neglected. . . . Oracy is central.' In this he specifically identified oral work as more important than reading or writing (literacy). The Bristol Association for the Teaching of English made a plea for regarding 'Spoken English as an essential subject which should have an important place in the school curriculum.'[16] The whole summer edition of the N.A.T.E. Bulletin was taken up with 'Some aspects of oracy'. The articles supported the importance of oral work but in particular in 'Speech in the school' James Britton made three very important statements which bore fruit in the theoretical framework of *Growth through English* and are taken up in more detail by Britton in later writings, especially *Language and Learning*:

1. English teachers do not have a skill to concern themselves with, a heritage to which they must lead the children but an area of experience with which to deal.
2. What gossip is doing is very similar to what the novel is doing. A great deal of our chat, our gossip, is language which is not participating in the world's affairs but which is sitting back and being a spectator of events. This is the spoken counterpart of literature.
3. Talk is a way by which each of us, for himself, structures experience.

The references to 'experience' echo other comments, the first one apparently referring to an area of *common* experience, the second to *personal* experience, though the distinction is not explicit. Here talk is the means whereby order is achieved; the work has to be done by ourselves and nothing is as potent as our own first-hand methods. The 'heritage' is discounted, perhaps because it offers ready-made solutions to other people's problems. Our own problems, our own unique experience requires our own unique solution. This primacy of the first-hand is further stressed in the view of literature as superior 'gossip', an idea which takes a similarity to be all that needs to be said. The distinctions between gossip and literature are apparently not as interesting. The parallel leads inevitably to either an enhanced value for 'gossip' or a less important place for literature.

In the years since the Dartmouth Seminar a great deal of agreement has been accorded to the nature of language as creative, by which we participate in the building of a perceived world. The stress is vital – our world is a creation of language to a large extent and we have to create our world as we learn our language. The two are contemporaneous. As Susanne Langer said, 'The fact is that our primary world of reality *is* a verbal one.'[17] Our early language is of course speech and it remains throughout our lives the mode we employ most. Thus far is there ground for the primacy of talk.

However, some serious qualifications need to be made. We do not create our world untrammelled. To an extent the world we create is already created in language and in the culture we imbibe. Our individual world is an adjustment between private and public. Language implies 'ours', implies 'shared'. Thus in looking at the way we 'structure experience' we must take account of much more than the personal viewpoint. Our native language structures experience through its syntax and vocabulary; the philosophical assumptions of the age structure experience; the attitudes to people, nature, birth, death, etc, which a culture takes structure the experience of anyone in that culture, through the symbolic forms, such as literature.

This whole area of what sociologists have called 'acculturation' has been bedevilled by a concentration on groups and sub-cultures, since this emphasis has pointed up the *restriction* of the choice of words and thus of world-view which is effected by the adoption of a culture. Certainly there are more restrictive cultures and less restrictive cultures but a rich culture (I am using a deliberately value-laden term) offers a range of possible worlds to create while at the same time making a larger number inaccessible. The richer the culture the wider the choice created. Talk alone however may lead us to accept a world that is restricted; indeed the very nature of talk is surely that it throws a man back on his private viewpoint and restricted perspective, like 'gossip'. It is in books that we retain a wealth of alternatives for consideration, a universal perspective. In literature especially do we find a multiplicity of worlds, of roles, of ways of living – a heritage, in fact.

Further, writing as a mode of language has two particular powers not available to speech – its power of inclusiveness and its power of coherence. By being preserved in symbolic form (writing) language can sustain thought far longer than speech, so that more of life can be embraced, put to the test for inclusion, related one part to another and made available beyond personal acquaintance. Thus, after all the talk of the Dartmouth Seminar, it was to a book that participants looked to tell them what they had experienced. Probably, until they read the book, most would not have developed a coherent picture of the important threads of the conference. Similarly, the Bullock Report is not just news for those who were not on the committee. It was, importantly, the attempt of the committee to tell itself what it thought.

We still have the *writings* of John Dewey, A. N. Whitehead, George Sampson, offering alternatives no amount of talk alone would come to. Talk is potent as exploratory structuring of experience – but it needs reading and writing alongside it to charge it with its full power.

Civilization begins anew

The second element in the child-centred theory of education asserts the view that each generation has new problems, a new world. I have already claimed that the heritage of culture is very much an active agent in the creation of the world. But David Holbrook in his paper 'Creativity in the English programme' for the Dartmouth Seminar[18] wrote 'civilization begins anew in every child'. There is no need to repeat the arguments already rehearsed for the *reciprocal* action of person and culture in the formation of 'civilization'. Here I want to draw on a figure depicted by Michael Oakeshott in his *Rationalism in Politics*; he sets out to describe the 'rationalist' in the following terms:

> He does not neglect experience but often appears to do so because he insists always upon it being his own experience (wanting to begin everything de novo). . . . He has no sense of the accumulation of experience, only of the readiness of experience when it has been converted into a formula; the past is significant to him only as an encumbrance. . . . Having cut himself off from the traditional knowledge of society, and denied the value of any education more extensive than a training in a technique of analysis, he is apt to attribute to mankind a necessary inexperience in all the critical moments of life, and if he were more self-critical he might begin to wonder how the race had ever succeeded in surviving. . . . [He] falls easily into the error of identifying the customary and the traditional with the unchanging. . . . The conduct of affairs for the Rationalist is a matter of solving problems.[19]

The rationalist is drawn to 'the politics of the *felt need*'. Now, there are influential elements of this kind of thinking in the stress in English teaching on the 'here and now' as against the 'there and then', the stress on the personal viewpoint, on experience, on relevance. There is in the figure described by Oakeshott a rejection of the relevance of the past to the life of the present that is implied in the idea that 'civilization begins anew in every child'. The odd thing is that in the thinking of the sixties it was quite common to find remarks about individuality, freshness, growth, needs, which were not related to the past in any precise way. It was as if the accepted idea of 'heritage' was totally discredited before John Dixon buried it in *Growth through English* and no more adequate version was yet possible – yet what is the contribution of the literature of the past without some idea of the relationship of the past with the present? Literature was often claimed as the centre of English teaching without any explicit rationale. It was an assumed value – and assumptions often go by default when circumstances change or when more dynamic or beguiling alternatives arise. The energy that has gone into expanding work on oracy, laudable in itself, has taken away from the energy needed to think out the complex uses of books. *Both* needed energetic thought.

Satisfying the Needs

Oakeshott pointed out the rationalist 'politics of the felt need'. If the relevance of the past is rejected by us as English teachers, if 'civilization begins anew in every child', there will be no wide perspective on the purposes of English, and there is unlikely to be any wide sense of value. What is important then is the life of the individual lived as he seeks. The only criteria available will be pragmatic, fragmentary. We can only go on what the child seems to need, and to express as need, however falteringly. The criteria of value are interest and efficacy. Sympathetic response from the child is taken to mean that his needs are being met; practical solutions are sought in the unique problems of a unique life.

John Dewey, father of progressive education wrote 'The proof of a good is found in the fact that the pupil responds; his response *is* use. His response to the material shows that the subject functions in his life.'[20] A view which would be warmly welcomed by many English teachers. Certainly a view commonly held in 1965–6 and at the Dartmouth Seminar. Its polar opposite was rarely expressed – that value is more than a personal thing and that many choices taken for interest and usefulness are misguided, even wrong. Teachers above all others cannot ignore that sad fact of life. The 'felt need' theory is sadly incomplete. It rests on an optimistic and dignified conception of humanity as essentially well-meaning and reasonable, which is fine as far as it goes. But it fails to account adequately for the need for the wisdom of experience and the past, or for the problems of immaturity and error. Thus we provide books we despise for children to enjoy; and when they do enjoy them, we persuade ourselves we have done some good.

Yet it *is* possible to posit the importance of concerning oneself as a teacher with the needs of a pupil without rejecting the perspective of one's culture. Everyone is unique but everyone also shares the staple diet of life's experiences, in facing which some understanding of possibilities gained from outside is helpful, even necessary. Literature does not offer simple solutions to problems but it does invite the reader to a variety of ways of 'structuring experience', some finer, subtler, more complex than our own. We need indeed to experience beyond the boundaries of our own existence if we are to understand the experience within it.

What I have been discussing are three aspects of a *child-centred* view of education, which Roland Harris, in an article in 1966,[21] saw as the root force behind 'the increasing pressure to accept a diffuse role' on the teacher. He detected in the Newsom Report and elsewhere a 'general movement in at least the theory of education towards a child-centred and outward-looking and away from a subject-centred organisation of the curriculum. . . . Again and again, successful teaching is seen as focused in the child himself, in his attitude to learning and in his growth as a mature person.' Further, Harris pointed 'All therapists have as their effective core the inter-personal relationship'.

If he was right about the character of the times, a number of questions would arise about English.

—*What* is English? What are its boundaries? Does it have any?

—Does the subject (any subject) matter? Is anything of value transmitted? (Often the answer had to be no).

—Aren't the relationships between the teacher and pupils more important than anything else? (The teacher must encourage the pupil to express his needs, which can then be satisfied).

The usefulness of Harris' article as an indicator of thinking in the sixties is not yet exhausted. He made a number of points which were live issues then, live issues at Dartmouth, and live issues still.

He continued, 'The boundaries of the (English teacher's) subject matter as taught in the schools . . . have become exceptionally ill-defined, or, if he is of an older generation, out of date'. The urge to include 'new' elements like talk had, it seems, outstripped the attempt at an all-embracing theory.

> The needs of the child, the teacher's respect for his own subject, and the demands of society and of the educational system as represented by the school structure and the content of examinations do not fit harmoniously together. . . . The generalization and diffusion of expectations may have created in the teacher of English a great uncertainty as to his role. . . . [The teaching of] the history of literature has become associated in the minds of some teachers of English with 'the handing out of secondhand opinions' and 'a complacent acquaintanceship with dead facts'. . . . The low verbal ability, and the cultural poverty of many pupils in a system of compulsory universal education has made it hard to find accepted works of prose literature which can in fact be read with understanding and enjoyment in the classroom.

The argument might have been from the puzzled teacher of English that if it were so hard perhaps it did not matter. Perhaps there were other, easier (i.e. more interesting to pupils) ways of teaching English, if we could only decide what it is that we are aiming at. If we are suffering from 'uncertainty' and lack of confidence perhaps it is because we are doing the wrong things with children. The uncertainty of aim would tend to encourage a move *towards* child-centredness, 'felt needs', as well as being, if Harris is right, to some extent *created by* the child-centredness.

Roland Harris seemed fairly certain about the uncertainty; David Holbrook does not write like one who is uncertain, then or now. His contribution to the theory of English teaching was of course well-established by 1965. His central work on English teaching was *English for Maturity*, a very influential book, speaking forcibly for the teachers in Secondary Modern Schools, but also outlining a rationale for the subject for teachers in any school. My own teaching was influenced and inspired by this book. Indeed it is one of the clutch of books that I still reread with profit. His ideas were in evidence in the journals of the following years and he attended the Dartmouth Seminar.

His basic case may be found in the following remarks: 'The more we read literature ourselves, the better sense we should gain of how rich life may and could be.' Compare this with his remark at Dartmouth 'Civilization begins anew in every child'. Wasn't there a tension in need of resolution? 'No two people are alike, to the despair of the commercial mind. Each human being has infinite capacities and infinite variations of spirit – and each life in time is a unique mystery.'[22]

This optimistic stress on the educability of *all* children into humane enlightenment by creative, imaginative work on literature and language was very powerful and invigorating. Holbrook was very clear about the important purposes of English teaching, the contribution of the writings of the past – to help with the personal problems of today – and the grounds for criticizing English through exercises. His confidence in the creativity of children was, however, related to his view of the role of literature as therapy (he was much impressed by psychotherapists such as Klein and Winnicott).

Here the child-centredness focuses on the *problem* of living. Living is a problem full of pitfalls, disasters and psychic mistakes. Inner order is the need of the child as of the man, and literature and creativity are the means to that order. In his remarks to the Dartmouth Seminar he said, 'Effective English teaching, in that it has to do with the whole complex of language in our lives, has to do with the whole problem of the individual identity and how it develops.'[23] Referring to practical skills of the kind sought by Heath and Barber he said, 'It is no good trying to develop "practical" uses of language unless we foster first of all an adequate capacity to be on good terms with oneself and to find inward order'. The centre lies within the child, who, from his efforts to solve his own psychic problems, will choose the appropriate steps more surely than a teacher could. However, 'From the experience of language art the child can be led to discover how other greater and finer adult minds have tackled the same inward problems as torment him and as he has tried to solve'. It is entirely characteristic of Holbrook's thinking that he uses 'torment' to depict the experience of living. Such a word flavours all his ideas and is indeed part of the urgency and power of his best writing.

The Need for a Theory of Development

A child-centred theory demands a theory of development. There are, according to the pattern chosen, various needs that ought to be met in education; Holbrook's view of essential development – his 'maturity' – has not been taken over very much by other writers. It is best expressed by his remark that 'we have a backlog of problems of inward structure and identity to work on'. Such a psychiatric role for English has been in the end found unsatisfactory by many – to anticipate the next chapter, Holbrook's influence at Dartmouth was not great. In the discussions following on from his paper delivered there the effort of the assembled delegates went into widening the idea of creativity beyond Holbrook's 'inward order and identity'. In the shift of theory this was one of the turning-points. Creativity was still thought to matter; personal and imaginative writing was important; literature had a place. But the reasons Holbrook advanced did not suit. The justification and purpose of creativity and literature had to be sought elsewhere if they were to be sought at all. Yet there was a vital element in Holbrook's offering which gave a dimension not taken up by John Dixon in *Growth through English*. Holbrook, drawing on the tradition of Arnold, Sampson, Thompson, Leavis, had a vision of human culture that was complex and impressive; life was a matter of some seriousness; a man could be dignified or disgraceful in his actions, honest or craven in his thinking. Maturity, then, was a normative concept in a way that 'growth' may not be. And Holbrook insisted on a critique of society as a context for his 'maturity'.

Other patterns of development were of interest – in the sixties the influence of Piaget and developmental psychology was strong. Could the stages of language development be identified? If they could, the task of the teacher was then apparently clear – to consolidate learning of an appropriate kind at each stage, allowing the process to work itself out naturally.

Such a pattern would provide a structure for teaching, and a rationale, though it would be of a different kind to that of Holbrook. It would tend towards the optimistic view that development to fullness is natural – only inhibiting, restricting factors will interrupt that development. It is a view supporting 'child-centred' approaches.

Frank Whitehead had already, before the Seminar, outlined in the first chapter of his book *The Disappearing Dais* an approach to teaching English based on 'maturation'. 'The term "maturation" is useful because it enables us to concentrate on the regularities of sequence which seem to be inescapable in all the circumstances and cultures we know of, and so to become aware of the limits within which the influence of the environment is bound to operate.'[24] The pattern of development offered guidelines to the most effective contribution of the teacher; it could even provide an aim. Whitehead developed these points further at Dartmouth. In Working Paper No. 2 'What is "continuity" in English teaching?'[25] he suggested 'we must look for our source of order in the inherent and inescapable sequence in the acquisition of a man's mother-tongue'.

This developmental pattern was adopted by the seminar, was central to John Dixon's book and provided an apparent bridge between language and literature, the child and the culture. It was akin to that implicit in James Britton's thinking. However since 'growth', 'maturation', 'development' are normally descriptive, value-free terms, such a rationale of education either assumes the inherent rightness of the child's urge to growth (or our indifference to the form taken by the growth) or requires that some criteria of value be found by which growth may be judged.

Frank Whitehead, though he did not amplify the point at Dartmouth, said that the role of English as a school subject is 'essentially, to foster, improve and refine the individual's ability to use the mother-tongue – to use it fully, flexibly, effectively, sensitively, and to use it for all the varied purposes which one's native language must serve in a modern civilized community. (Literature falls within this province because the creative and imaginative uses of language are an integral part of the life-experience of a civilized human being.)'

The end of growth is a 'civilized human being'. But this crucial point was not developed. However in *The Disappearing Dais* he had written a long and detailed chapter on 'Reading and literature' in which he developed a non-authoritarian approach to reading. He carefully described a teaching style that was not didactic (not insisting that the book was merely to be transmitted) but very much leading the child into understanding through sharing and enjoying. Nor did he insist that only the acknowledged classics were suitable.

He first addressed himself to the nature of the reading process, which he stressed 'was essentially a rethinking of the ideas on the printed page. . . . Reading is above all a "thought-getting process, involving at all stages the recognition by the reader of the important elements of meaning in their essential relations".' These words, quoted from the *36th Year Book of the National Society for the Study of Education, 1937*, stress the necessary discipline of the reader, the need to 'rethink' actively and creatively what the writer sought to say. In Whitehead's own words: '"Learning to read" has . . . to be seen as a continuing process which goes on throughout the child's school career, and which sets as its goal the power to read with understanding, appreciation and enjoyment – the power, in fact, to recreate as fully and accurately as possible the experience which lies embodied in the words on the printed page.'

The benefits to children of wide reading consisted of 'an extension of the capacity for experience, an enlargement and refinement of that imaginative grasp of the realities of human living and a deeper insight into the ways in which human beings (including ourselves) think and feel and behave and affect one another'.

It was this kind of belief, this kind of approach, that characterized my own teaching, seeking to match enjoyment and a disciplined attention, balancing the needs of the child with the essential demands of the achieved work of the mature writer, though it was not Frank Whitehead who first persuaded me of it. These were the ideas in the air at the time that I took to myself, above all from the *Use of English*. They were almost axiomatic, not really in question, but in Frank Whitehead's book they seemed to me what oft I'd thought, but ne'er so well expressed.

He also expressed a connexion between the life of the book and the life of the human being reading it that was part and parcel of my own mental luggage at that time. '. . . the quality of the imaginative experience we derive from our books has a close bearing upon the quality of experience we are capable of in our everyday living.'

I was attempting in my teaching to increase the child's capacity for full living, through a lively but controlled subjection to the book. Give and take were both essential, a reciprocal imprinting.

Another aim was to encourage in the child a developing evaluative stance, capable of judging while experiencing what lay 'embodied in the words'. This I found difficult, since the interested pupil is inclined to adopt too readily the views of the adult, without the effort of going through all the stages of the judgment. To pretend to no views was worse than useless; to assert was often to short-circuit the slow growth to independent, sensitive discrimination.

Frank Whitehead saw the danger: '. . . the hard fact is that it is only the method of judging that can be learnt, not the judgments themselves. Certainly we must never forget that the pupil's own genuine, independent and first-hand judgment is the only one that really counts.' He did, however, insist that the effort must be made. 'No one can be said to have fully mastered the art of reading until he is able not only to take in the meaning of what he reads but also to assess its worth . . . questions of relative value will always be there in the background of good English teaching at any stage.'

I have detailed Frank Whitehead's approach to literature both to indicate the nature of thinking that was available to teachers of English before the Dartmouth Seminar, but also to show how an attempt was being made to develop two incompletely resolved central features, 'literature' or 'language'. A maturational theory of development would tend towards the latter, though efforts were being made to provide an all-embracing account. Thus Alan Davies spoke of 'a whole range of sub-languages, of varieties, of registers, of which literature is only one and a highly specialized one'.[26] Nancy Martin, a colleague of James Britton at the University of London, and subsequently director of the series of projects looking at writing, sought in 1965 'a unifying theory' and suggested that the mother-tongue might be the source of that unity. 'Philosophical studies on the nature of the symbolizing processes in language and thought have "placed" literature in the general context of language operating on individuals in society.'[27]

At the same time Peter Doughty was, in writing about poetry, torn between the orthodoxy of 'poetry is the centre' and 'talk has come to have a central place'.[28] Such self-contradiction illustrates very well the ambiguity of 'central' and the unresolved contradictions in the ideas of the time The sufficiency of literature was just on the point of being challenged.

In concluding this brief survey of the thinking of the early sixties, it seems possible to extract from the complex picture the following problems taxing minds before Dartmouth:

—What constitutes the subject English?

—Where lie the important co-ordinating features (its 'centre')?

—What is the relationship between language and literature?

—What is the relationship between the unique child and the culture into which he comes?

—Is there any source to which we should look for a developmental structure in English teaching?

They were also the open questions which taxed the delegates to the Dartmouth Seminar and there were high hopes that the collection of highly respected authorities in the field of English teaching assembled could make progress towards answering them.

Chapter 2

Dartmouth and *Growth through English*

When we mean to build
We first survey the plot, then draw the model,
And when we see the figure of the house
Then must we rate the cost of the erection
Which if we find outweighs ability
What do we do then but draw anew the model
In fewer offices?

Henry IV pt 2

To many teaching English today the Dartmouth Seminar of 1966 will seem like ancient rather than recent history; many will perhaps fail to see any point in looking at such a gathering, distant in time and place, because they feel it has had no influence on their own teaching. Why then go back to a conference held so long ago; many of those assembled then would not be known by many now?

There is nevertheless a historical connection. Those assembled were the 'progressive cutting-edge" of English teaching then, virtually all those who were contributing to a search for a coherent, all-embracing account of English and who were therefore going to influence or be involved with any developments at large. Virtually all the major figures influential since then were present and were influential there. The seminar was not revolutionary, but it can be seen now to have had a substantial effect on the drift of change.

The Anglo-American Dartmouth Seminar was brought together in the belief that 'English as a school subject was facing a series of critical problems both in the United States and in the United Kingdom' and that 'an international exchange of experience and opinion would be helpful in arriving at solutions and in suggesting lines of future international collaboration'.[29] Whether the sense of crisis was as strong in this country as it was in America is doubtful, though undoubtedly there was a certain ferment, an energetic formulation of questions. Perhaps the hopes from international perspectives were born of wishful thinking, for it is hard to see just how such a conference could help problems derived from different traditions, different cultures. The mother-tongue is primarily national, not international and the 'sense of frustration and futility' which H. J. Muller observed at Dartmouth demonstrates this hard fact.[30]

27

Certainly the frequent reference in the various accounts of the Seminar testify to real difficulties in agreeing on the meaning of words, of recognizing common problems, of defining agreed recommendations. Muller 'wearied at times of the continual clashing of half-truths . . . It was difficult at times to isolate areas of common agreement as a starting point for a broad reconciliation of views . . . The British and Americans were deeply divided by a common language; and . . . the entire conference was shattered into myriad pieces by a common subject and discipline.'

On the other hand John Dixon nowhere records such impressions of incomprehension and confusion but rather 'the excitement and intellectual satisfaction of having just seen a major issue resolved'.[31] It seems that there are two incompatible views of what happened, dependent to an extent on the spectator's evaluation of what came out of it. Denys Thompson for example felt 'the seminar seems now to have made little progress because it was too much given to pretentious intellectualizing' and recalled 'the seminar's unwillingness to come to grips with the issues presented by the more relevant papers' and explained that 'conditions and personnel militated against any effective exchange'.[32] Those who felt on the other hand that what emerged was of value, such as James Britton, clearly felt the process was also a stimulating and enlivening one.

For something coherent did emerge. A reading of the volumes of papers produced at Dartmouth does lead to some fairly clear answers to the following questions:

—What were the basic questions being asked there?
—What issues were considered most important?
—What directions were taken in the search for answers?

There was a corporate drift, under pressure from its individual voices, as a result of which added impetus was given to some possible lines of development and not to others. Some voices were discouraged; others were lauded, encouraged to further a point and it is not fanciful to see that the voices which were encouraged – not regarded as incomprehensible, parochial or quirky – have been encouraged to take the centre of the stage more energetically since the Seminar. (Dixon, Barnes and Britton seem to have gained an audience; Whitehead, Thompson and Holbrook did not. The Seminar could not relate their offerings to the total picture, the 'map' as it was persistently called.)

What emerged was *Growth through English* by John Dixon (who had been commissioned by N.A.T.E to write a report) and *The Uses of English* by H. J. Muller. (The latter is almost unknown to British readers, though it provides sometimes a corrective, albeit journalistic, viewpoint to Dixon's.)

Growth through English was an avowedly 'partial report' in which Dixon sought to stress 'the consensus that emerged' and thus underplayed 'the dissenting views that tended to become submerged in the excitement of our agreement'.[33] The consensus was clearly one with which he agreed but nevertheless it is true, as he claimed, that his book was 'a tissue of quotations' from the papers of the Seminar. In considering the book, I want to look in particular at three aspects:

—What were the issues selected as important by the conference?

—Was there any significant personal selection in John Dixon's account? (Any omissions, particularly?)

—What, critically, can be made of the particular picture Dixon gave?

A look at the topics and titles of the papers at Dartmouth shows a considerable overlap with the issues felt to be important in Britain in the years before.

Working Papers were submitted and discussed on:

1. What is English? (content)
2. What is 'continuity' in English teaching? (sequence and structure)
3. One road or many? (a consideration of setting and individual treatment for the unique child)
4. Knowledge and proficiency in English (content and aims)
5. Standards and attitudes (dialect, language of children).

Study Groups concerned themselves with:

1. The spoken word
2. Drama
3. Creativity
4. How does a child learn English?
5. Response to literature
6. Myth
7. The role of technological innovation in the English classroom
8. The place of linguistics
9. External examinations
10. The implications of an 'audio-visual' world.

Of course we should expect some echoes of the British concerns since some of the same people were at the Seminar. However not all the issues received equal attention, as Denys Thompson pointed out. The first paper 'What is English'[34] sought crucially to account for what should be in and what should be out of the subject English. Delivered by an American, Albert Kitzhaber, it excluded etiquette and 'social slops' (the U.S. had experienced a more voracious inclusiveness than the U.K.); Kitzhaber quoted a linguist H. L. Gleason on a point of crucial importance: 'English must have a centre about which it can integrate – a centre of such significance that it can overcome the centrifugal forces clearly at work to dismember the field of English.'[35] He then considered literature as the centre, asking whether we could 'accurately define the central or organizing principles of literature, for these will affect not only sequence but content and approach'. However, as the most satisfactory formulation he suggested the following: 'language must be the integrating centre, about which a new curriculum is to be built'.

Muller in his report saw in this part of the conference a choice actively being considered, between the centrality of literature, which many teachers regard as the very heart of the subject, and language, for 'other teachers believe that English should be centred on language – the understanding manipulation and appreciation of language'. This can be seen as a continuation of the debate in the letter columns in the *Use of English*.

Following the paper from Kitzhaber, the Chairman of the session, Douglas Barnes, said 'our main task is to find some conceptual pattern whereby all of our different approaches may be placed on the same map, and not the impossible task of coming to an agreement between such a large number of different people'. This seems a very sensible Chairman's remark, setting a realistic target to enable discussion to proceed, but the notion of a *map*, a full coverage of all the territory in their relative positions, was taken up more ambitiously by John Dixon in his account of *models*. Both metaphors are characteristic of his book but it must be pointed out that the limited function of a 'map' to a Chairman is very different to the use of a map which tells us where we *ought* to go. I shall return to the models and map shortly.

James Britton replied to Albert Kitzhaber in a paper which can be seen in retrospect to have effectively persuaded the Seminar to take its offered direction. (It was the pattern to have a 'respondent' to each paper.) Britton doubted the validity of the question 'What is English?' but sought to present an answer in a recognition that 'the function of language' is 'something more than is suggested by the skills of communication'.[36] 'We need to ask "What is the function of the mother-tongue in learning?" . . . What we want . . . is an operational view of language, an operational view of the teaching of the mother-tongue.'[37]

And after an account of his scheme for language uses from the 'spectator' to the 'participant' role he said 'I suggest that the area in which language operates in English lessons is that of personal experience, in other words – the relation between the ego and the environment' and here clearly was the role of literature (or as he designated it 'language in the spectator role') for literature is about 'the relationships in which the human quality of the emotional relationship is a part of what is afoot'.

Here literature was given an importance but it was within a language schema that it got its *raison d'être*. Literature was *part* of language – a point of view which was converted by John Dixon into the 'map'. The 'map' is, essentially, 'language'. James Britton at that time saw English as being concerned with the 'spectator' role – i.e. one important aspect of language – but once the language schema is accepted as valid it will almost inevitably lead to a feeling that the range of language uses in English lessons should be expanded, and literature only one among many. (Such has been the evolving viewpoint of Britton himself.) This schema is of course largely value-free; it does not say which are less important uses. It just shows there are *different* ones – any criterion of value must come from outside it.

In effect, the case for the centrality of literature had been given up and the reason may be that Britton's schema could become a map on which 'all of our different approaches may be placed'. It enabled all the disparate voices, from linguists to professors of English Literature, academics to teachers, to *go on talking to each other*, while yet postponing questions of value, which would lead to disharmony. That is not to say that the schema was considered valuable only for that reason. It was of course a more high-flown categorization of the conceptions of language already available. For example, Frank Whitehead's view of language as the 'medium in which we have evolved our most deeply-ingrained modes of interpreting the universe in which we live; and our capacity for human relationships, our ways of perceiving, understanding and mastering the phenomena of our everyday existence are shaped and coloured by it in countless ways.'[38] The particular character of his view leads to high relative valuation for literature; Britton's in the end to equality *inter pares*.

In a 'Report to seminar' after the discussion the point was made that 'We wish to reject the idea of literature as a content which can be "handed over" to the pupils, and to emphasize instead the idea of literature as contributing to the sensitivity and responsibility with which they live through language'.

What did John Dixon make of this discussion in his report? He made a map 'on which the confusing claims and theories can be plotted'[39] and placed on the map three 'models' of English – whether 'theory' or 'practice' is not clear and his treatment varied from model to model.

Models

Now, a 'model' is a replica which is simplified so that it is recognisably similar to the original, but it cannot do all the things the original can do. It is reduced to handling proportions. As such its uses are limited and one must of course beware trying to do with it what was possible with the original. These truisms preface a consideration of John Dixon's 'models', which were made to carry a great weight by him, to make out a case which proved to be very persuasive and influential. Since the models were used loosely to impel an argument for a particular theory of English teaching, it is necessary to examine them in some detail.

The 'map' of the three 'models' of English teaching was as far as I am aware John Dixon's own, distilled from the assumptions and compromises of the discussion at the Seminar. (He described them as 'singled out' in discussion.) There is no evidence in the papers of their origin. He described them as an 'historical' dimension – 'the first centred on *skills*: it fitted an era when *initial* literacy was the prime demand'. The second model 'stressed the *cultural heritage*, the need for a civilizing and socially unifying content'. And the third model, which he described as 'current', 'focuses on *personal growth*: on the need to re-examine the learning processes and the meaning to the individual of what he is doing in English lessons'. Of these three the earlier ones were 'limited' and needed to be 'reinterpreted'.

Thus far the argument seems simple and acceptable. The first conception of English *is* oversimple, the second leaves many questions unanswered, the third recognizes that education requires a *learner*. However in following his discussion of the models one by one, grave doubts arise about the weight being placed on these simple structures. The first is the easiest target; the main onslaught being the charge that teaching 'skills' omits so much of value in the use of English that it is restrictive. (It is clear here that what Dixon had in mind is English by exercises, the very beast hunted by Thompson, Heath and others in the years before Dartmouth.) As a conception of English teaching it is inadequate.

Dixon accounted for this model 'historically' as we have seen. It arose to meet a need, he inferred. Yet if it was still alive and kicking perhaps there was some reason, some purpose it served in some small degree. Having cut it down to size Dixon salvaged nothing. He moved on to model number two – 'cultural heritage' – which he claimed 'was clearly intended to fill the vacuum left by the skills model' – a statement of very doubtful historical accuracy. This was a very wayward account indeed of the thinking of Arnold, Sampson, or the many others who have propounded the importance of conveying the riches of our culture to our pupils; their impetus came from a full sense of the worth of the culture, not as a solution to a curriculum problem. He mentioned Arnold and the 1919 Newbolt Report as creators in part of this 'vision', which was not examined at all as a *theory*, a set of intentions, in the way one would expect, given the nature of the enterprise. Instead we were given a very sad and it must be admitted all too accurate account of 'the betrayal of this vision' in 'a series of inky marginal annotations and essay notes'.

His most searching criticism was levelled at the idea of 'culture as a *given*' which he presented as a flaw in the theory, when it might be more true to see it as a flaw in one version. He then made a remark which would be agreed to happily by many who see themselves as 'transmitters of cultural heritage' – 'What is vital is the interplay between his (the child's) personal world and the world of the writer: a teacher must acknowledge both sides of the experience, and know both of them intimately if he is to help to bring the two into a fruitful relationship.'

To which we would say 'amen' and even add that that is exactly the point of 'culture' and 'heritage'. However the 'average teacher' had betrayed this 'vision' by his emphasis on the written word and the presentation of 'experience (fiction) to his pupils, rather than drawing from them their experience (of reality and the self)'.

Now the 'average teacher' is a dreadful weapon with which to beat any theory; the use of 'rather than' points to a caricature – an either/or argument of dubious merit. What, if that is what 'the average teacher' makes of the theory, are we to make of the contribution of, for example, Denys Thompson, who seems to have spent his life applauding the value of literature as our inheritance, while yet stressing the need for 'a fruitful relationship'. It is as if the *Use of English* had never been published, its consistent attempt to bring together culture and child never made. Within the Seminar there was abundant complex life in the idea of cultural heritage from Thompson himself, Frank Whitehead, Glyn Lewis and others – why this dismissal?

Perhaps it was that John Dixon saw in his 'cultural heritage' model the approach to teaching literature which had been much criticized by Frank Whitehead particularly but largely with the endorsement of the whole English contingent – the teaching of knowledge *about* literature. Literature and reading were discussed in great detail at the Seminar and throughout there was a strong resistance among the British contingent to a codified, ordered instruction *about* literature in favour of a concern with personal response. But that is not at all the same as a rejection of the cultural heritage.

There clearly was a kind of literature teaching which deserved criticism. Unfortunately John Dixon suffered from a too simple theoretical construct, so that teaching literature in such a way that both the book and the child had safeguarded legitimate rights was given no theoretical foundation, no place in the new pantheon. If there is any place where John Dixon was guilty of historical discontinuity it is here. As a result many teachers could find no place in the new thinking and were condemned either to eccentricity or dishonesty.

The influence of this dismissal of model number two has been great, especially under a thoroughgoing concentration on the child as centre as defined in his third model – 'personal growth'. It has indeed been used since then to support a rationalist rejection of the past, as available to us in literature, but which is not felt to be relevant to us here and now. This in spite of the tradition of 'fruitful relationship' between child and culture already available.

The critique of the caricature was justly done, but the caricature missed out so much truth. This was a fundamental flaw in the first chapter, which unhinged the whole book. The inadequacy of treatment was to some extent due of course to his excitement at a more complex, more adequate model elsewhere, to which he is more sympathetic because it stressed the child rather than the culture. The idea of the 'fruitful relationship' was in fact forgotten for a child-centred theory of an unbalanced kind, though it was based largely on conceptions shared widely at the time.

The remarks of John Dewey on the curriculum are useful here.

> The fundamental factors in the educative process are an immature undeveloped being; and certain aims, meanings, values incarnate in the matured experience of the adult. The educative process is the due interaction of these forces. . . .
>
>   But here comes the effort of thought. It is easier to see the conditions in their separateness . . . than to discover a reality to which each belongs. . . . When this happens a really serious practical problem – that of interaction – is transformed into an unreal and hence insoluble, theoretic problem. Instead of seeing the educative process steadily and as a whole, we see conflicting terms. We get the case of the child *vs* the curriculum; of the individual nature *vs* social culture. [40]

John Dixon seems to have attempted 'a reality to which each belongs' but largely because of his treatment of the 'cultural heritage model', risked creating an either/or theory. In fact he fell into the very danger he identified earlier – 'over-rejection'.

In outlining his third model, more adequate, more 'current', John Dixon, as we might expect, developed it more fully. He began with 'the need to build English teaching . . . on our observation of language in operation from day to day' and produced for the reader some writing of a ten-year-old boy, as an example of children using language 'for their own purposes'.

The piece of writing convincingly illustrated a writer with 'something worth sharing' with 'a sympathetic and interested listener'. Dixon over-stated the freedom from influence of the piece, but showed with conviction that attention to skills alone would not produce writing 'for the primary purpose in language, to share experience'. Nor would the heritage model help 'because it neglects the most fundamental aim of language – to promote interaction between people'. This was a very tendentious remark which he did not stay with throughout his book; nor could he, for there are other claimants for 'the most fundamental' aim, such as 'making meanings for oneself'. (It seems a mistake to seek *one* as crucial.)

D. W. Harding wrote 'language and experience interpenetrate one another. The language available to us influences our experience at intimate levels and if we manage to convey experience precisely, that may be due partly to the fact that available modes of expression were influencing the experience from the start',[41] which I take to be showing expression as the result of the necessary interaction of individual and culture.

Dixon seems to have shot wide of the mark in his eagerness to hit at the use of literature as model for imitation. As a result he failed to understand the interaction that is necessary for meaningful expression (or self-definition). However he did show that there are many purposes in using language 'recalling experience, getting it clear, giving it shape and making connections, speculating and building theories, celebrating (and exorcising) particular moments'. This wide range was seen to justify the recognition of children's writing *as literature* – his study of the pieces quoted was couched in such terms, an approach taken up later more fully. Nowhere in his account of the third model did he inter-relate the culture and the child – we were presented with an image of a child seeking alongside others to fulfil his own felt needs.

He did recognize dangers in his theorizing (which he would claim to be an account of actual teaching approaches). The first one – over-rejection – he was guilty of. The second was over-simplification to which he had already, it seems, succumbed in his image of 'growth'. 'As people we exist and assert ourselves in response to our world (our family, neighbourhood, teachers). The sense of our own reality is bound up with our sense of theirs, and both intimately depend on an aware-ness built up through language.'

Literature, for John Dixon 'by bringing new voices into the class-room, adds to the store of shared experience. Each pupil takes from the store what he can and what he needs.' That is, not finer voices, better voices – just new to the pupil. Presumably then, if the voices are not what the pupil needs he does not listen; he uses them as he wishes; he is the sole arbiter of right use. If this is a caricature, it is one *allowed* by the theory put forward.

Conclusion
What in effect John Dixon's first chapter did – it was his intention –
was to set at the centre of English the use of language in operation to
create our own world. Literature and reading were given a contributory,
ancillary role. Talking and writing (expression rather than impression)
took their place. Though the case was presented tendentiously (e.g. the
'average teacher' was not allowed to soil his preferred model) it has
been influential on teachers. The very shift in theory he made in the
first chapter was the shift of the decade, though it did not originate
there.

Literature

The Seminar did take a protracted look at literature when it set up a
Study Group on the subject 'Response to literature'. The group was
first addressed by James Britton, who offered the notion that 'the proper
response to a work of literature is . . . to share in the author's satisfaction
that it was as it was and not otherwise . . . much of the satisfaction in
most literature comes from a contemplation of the form given to
events. . . . Since the response of children is unformed but similar to
that of an adequate adult response, teaching is a matter of leading on to
the adequate ones, not eradicating the child's. . . . Our aim should be to
refine and develop responses the children are already making.'[42]
However Britton's account of the *nature* of response was eccentric and
has not been taken up anywhere else. Certainly this feature was not
developed at all at Dartmouth. 'Development can best be described as
an increasing sense of form.' He saw response as a very self-conscious
awareness of an artefact, which it is hard to see as the important
element in response at an adult or juvenile level.

A feature more influential in Britton's contribution came when
he offered 'an unorthodox way of defining literature which has the
advantage of placing it among linguistic activities generally . . .
literature as a particular kind of utterance – an utterance that a writer
has "constructed", not for use but for his own satisfaction'. That is, it is
language in the 'spectator' role. And as a gloss 'When we speak the
language, the nearest name I can give it is "gossip"; when we write it, it
is literature'. So, obviously, 'What a child writes is of the same order as
what the poet or novelist writes and is valid for the same reasons'.

Britton's self-consciousness in presenting an 'unorthodox' view
should be noted – since it is nowadays regarded as orthodoxy. The view
clearly reiterated the attempt earlier in the Seminar and before to place
literature among 'language uses', which might lead to a useful conceptual framework if the assumptions on which it is based are sound.

However just as Britton's description of response as 'increasing sense of form' are partial and even tangential to the real interaction between book and reader, so the idea of literature being quintessentially constructed 'for his own satisfaction' took one of the psychological functions of writing and made it the significant one on which to build a theory. What was so wrong with this is that it denied any seriousness to writing, which was 'author-centred', egocentric and so not really important. Certainly if that is the truth about literature then what a child writes *is* literature and not only because they are both 'in the spectator role'. Britton ignored the nature of literature as something created 'out there' with a life of its own to be drawn out by the reader and sees it as merely the act of a writer.

The eccentric inadequacy of Britton's paper is apparently reflected in the fact that there was very little extended study given to most of his ideas subsequently. The exception was the underlying theory of 'spectator' language, which, as John Dixon reported, provided the background to all the thinking on literature. Most of the following papers were concerned with the tactics and sequence of teaching literature, confirming Muller's impression that 'the consensus stood basically for literature for its own sake, as its own reward. . . . Everyone appeared to take for granted the case for it, to feel no need of either attacking or justifying its traditionally high place in the English curriculum.'[43]

There were however two interesting papers given to this Study Group. First, 'Cultural heritage' by Denys Thompson and James Squire (Appendix III, 'Response to literature') and second 'Response and formulation' by Barbara Hardy and Wallace Douglas (Appendix IV).

There is dramatic irony to be had in reading Appendix III. The very title is inclined to prick the attention after reading of John Dixon's three models. Oddly, in view of that account, what Thompson and Squire offered was that 'cultural heritage' is 'not a packet to be transmitted inert. It is alive and changing; each generation takes from it what it needs and in its turn adds to it.' In any account of a 'cultural heritage model' of teaching there ought surely to be some consideration of the *nature* of cultural heritage – John Dixon was antipathetic to that. Characteristically, he refused in his report any place for the question: 'Without contact with his literary heritage, can any American be an American, or an Englishman an Englishman?'[44]

The paper submitted by Douglas and Hardy, 'Response and Formulation' went some way to doing what Britton's paper did not do. They sought to pin precisely the nature of the interaction between reader and read.

In the transaction of comprehending a literary work . . . the facts are as they are in part because of the way in which they may be modified by the response they cause in students.

A recognition that there is a complex interplay in response, not merely receptive-ness. . . . we want to suggest that works of art are by no means so separate from us as human perceivers. . . . Of course there is something 'out there' . . . Hence there ought to be no suggestion that 'response' in our usage refers to anything free-floating or merely emotional.

The role of the teacher was seen 'as one who directs, or at least leads a process by which students achieve feeling comprehensions of various works of art'. The authors recognized 'a natural movement from subject to object and back again'. However, in any situation of difficulty the test of a good teacher of literature should be his willingness to sacrifice the integrity of the poem in the concern for the student, indicating again a generally 'child-centred' approach (though crucially modified by a need to achieve 'feeling comprehension'). These two papers offer a decided counter-balance to Britton's stress on literature as writing, both tending to recognition of literature as achievement demanding attentive as well as creative reading. If we look at John Dixon's account of the Seminar's deliberations we see he has accepted as completely satisfactory the notion of language 'in the role of spectator'. In Chapter 2 of *Growth through English*, 'Processes in language learning', he said 'The role of spectator – of an attentive, immersed onlooker – is thus a link between the child and the artist'. This link held together all that he had to say later about reading but first he asserted 'we become aware of the work children have to do (through language) before they can draw on the mature writer' giving a primacy to the expressive modes of language. (Though in fact in the acquisition of language the 'impressive' listening and reading do not *wait on* the others. They proceed together.) Accepting the connection of gossip and literature suggested by Britton he said, 'it is at the level of gossip that we all start' a remark of staggering over-simplification. His ground was laid, and when he came to 'An analysis of activities in class' he naturally placed 'Talk and drama' before 'Writing and reading' (note, writing before reading). His purpose was to describe the setting, the context for language development through operant uses, to which literature is seen to make some contribution. Drama was 'central to English work at every level'. In the work of developing language the classroom was 'a language community'. (Isn't there an important one which subsumes the classroom – a culture?) Writing allowed the children to 'enjoy shaping their world'.

Dixon was rightly very wary of giving children ready-made forms to put on and work through. If personal experience is the matter of

English, the English teacher should not forget the immense range that there is. 'The English specialist is often tempted to restrict himself to looking at life through fictions – quite forgetting that one can also look at people and situations direct'. Such restrictive foolishness exists but the naïve conception of the interrelation of life and literature ('fictions') that was assumed ignored all the line of thought that had been defended by G. W. Dennis in his letter to *Use of English* – 'art for life's sake'. Dixon acknowledged a connection between 'life as it is enacted and life as it is represented' but did not conceive of our reading as having a major impact on our way of seeing the world, though oddly he seemed to believe that our *language* might. This in spite of his quoting from D. W. Harding 'If we could obliterate the effects on a man, at the occasions when he was 'merely a spectator' it would be profoundly to alter his character and outlook.' Presumably the generalized role of the spectator is what matters, not any particular kind – such as literature (adopting Dixon's framework here for the moment). This is borne out by Dixon's subsequent remark that 'a wide definition of literature was used throughout the Seminar'. Leaving aside the recognition that such a wide definition might have been a useful conference step, like constructing 'maps', we can see that the conception of language in the role of spectator would lead to the belief that 'when pupils' stories and poems, though necessarily private activities, re-emerge as experience to be shared and talked over with teachers and classmates, they become the literature of the classroom'.

Such an acceptance of pupils' work as 'embryonic literature' had immense implications for the contribution of adult literature. It becomes grist to the mill of personal experience and as such may be rejected or accepted on whether or not it impinges on whatever personal preoccupations the pupil has at the moment. There was no question, here, of literature as something 'out there' to which we must give 'feeling comprehension'.

I would not wish to suggest that Dixon did not support the development of reading – only that the particular framework he selected from the Seminar and presented in his book stressed the *personal* side of reading at the expense of what the book requires (attentiveness); a stress that inevitably fed the use of literature for any personal purpose. He did however give signs of appreciating literature 'for its own sake'. 'Many of the great *texts* become *experiences* in reading. . . . We look to literature to bring order and control to our world, and perhaps to offer an encounter with difficult areas of experience. . . . Literature invites us into ways of evaluating aspects of life *as* we experience them.'

But 'our sense of the role of spectator came to define the term "literature" in our discussions'. This was clearly the most powerful influence on the conception of literature, for as part of the total flow of activity in English lessons literature served other needs. 'The essential talk that springs from literature is talk about experience – as *we* know it and *he* sees it . . . only in a classroom where talk explores experience is literature drawn into the dialogue – otherwise it has no place.'

There was no value accepted here for private reading – only 'talk about experience' validated reading. A curious belief but in the end an influential one when allied to a rationalist creation of a new start and an indifference to literature as an achievement to be recognized. If literature is a 'centre' for English in Dixon's terms it is a centre *from which* the pupils move. 'The *writing* that springs from literature takes us in two directions: outwards into our own shaping of experience, tapped and activated by our reading – and that is the usual direction – or in towards the writer's experience, sifting and savouring the thing for itself – and that is rarer.'

The selection that Dixon made of the voices at Dartmouth is strikingly clear. What he consistently omitted from his 'map' were any that looked to a tradition, a transmission, a developed collection of values, for these were inert, moribund. Growth and life were to be found only in the person. This selection meant not only that the voices of Thompson and Squire were ignored, those of Douglas and Hardy transmuted; the contribution of Glyn Lewis was as if it had never been, in marked contrast to Muller's book, which allows him a voice.

'Glyn Lewis could sound like a voice crying in the wilderness as he alone[45] kept insisting on the claims of our heritage.' Lewis' main contribution was in his paper 'The teaching of English' given to Working Party IV as part of their considerations. (Their subject was 'Knowledge and proficiency in English'.) He sought to balance the personal dimension of education against the public.

'Though education is an individual and personal process it is not simply subjective, but proceeds in certain observable and objective ways.'[46] And as an important example 'A child needs to be induced to want to judge not simply the interest of a point of view or opinion but whether in fact it is reasonably likely to be true and to judge the relevance of an experience for the task of daily living.'

The grounds for this case were that 'The child's development is a process of learning within a particular culture'. Lewis went on:

> Clearly we must recognize the importance of the instinct of origination, but an education based on the training of this instinct is not enough. Language conveys to a child an already prepared system of values and ideas that form his culture.

> Each new generation is not a new people; we are what we are because we are able to share a past, in a common heritage, not simply because of our ability to communicate in the present and share the excitement of innovation.

I believe there can be no adequate theory of the teaching of the mother-tongue without some attempt at a theory of culture (and Lewis was making an attempt). The bizarre aspect of Dixon's book is that he didn't present one, leaving his theory rootless, unable to account for any purpose or aim in teaching English.

On a whole series of issues the conference was united, to such an extent that there was little discussion required and no evidence of dissent. Thus, streaming was undesirable; the influence of examinations was probably harmful and should be studied; drama had an important place in English; children should be encouraged to write creatively (though Holbrook's psychotherapy was put onto a side-track). That this agreement was 'achieved' was perhaps due to an underlying agreement that each child is unique but the processes of growth fall into a pattern. The whole Seminar, it appears, was arranged on the American side as a parallel to the Woods Hole Conference of 1959 out of which came the idea of Bruner's 'Spiral' sequential curriculum. Such hopes were demonstrated in the subject of the second Working Party – 'Continuity in English'. The hopes were that some structured sequence would emerge, which could guide the construction of a curriculum. The U.S. delegates sought structure in the *subject* – in the content. The U.K. representatives however, led by Frank Whitehead, looked to the *processes* of maturation and growth to supply the underlying sequence of a curriculum.

He suggested that 'we must look for our source of order in the inherent and inescapable sequence in the acquisition of a man's mother-tongue'.[47] This of course was a repetition of his espousal of 'maturation' in his book *The Disappearing Dais* and although the Americans were at first baffled by the rejection of the example set by Bruner and later hostile to Whitehead's child-centred structure, they never mounted a coherent alternative. The view of English as the learning of the mother-tongue was certainly common ground to teachers and linguistics experts alike and probably provided a basis for continuing discussion.

Whitehead outlined his view of English teaching as fostering, improving and refining 'the individual's ability to use his mother-tongue – to use it flexibly, effectively, sensitively and to use it for all the varied purposes which one's native language must serve in a modern civilized community'. Such a description stressed width and variety (the forces for inclusion) and the word 'civilized' meant little more probably than 'advanced'. Nor was any guidance given as to the more important purposes. Rather, coping with the demands of the community was seen as the minimum aim. However he contined: 'Literature falls within this province because the creative and imaginative uses of language are an integral part of the life-experience of a civilized human being.' 'Civilized' meant much more now, implying some level of culture, some quality of life. As such it implied some uses of the mother-tongue were especially important, while yet remaining 'part' of the whole language development. At the same time it inferred that productive uses of 'creative and imaginative' language (writing and speaking) were valuable, as well as receptive uses (reading and literature).

This made an instructive comparison with John Dixon's final report for he nowhere offers us a glimpse of the end of the processes of growth. Instead, we were to seek to know more certainly how growth proceeds (research was the hope) that we may enable it, not restrict it. Frank Whitehead in his paper drew upon such evidence as there was available as to the stages of growth in language, most of it concerned with the early years, the initial steps. He warned that 'it may often by peculiarly difficult to distinguish between those aspects of the observable sequence which are tied to a particular environment and those regularities which seem to be inescapable in all the cultures we know of'. This warning would seem to apply most to the secondary school years where we have little coherent evidence of sequence and maturation. Whitehead picked out some 'dimensions of growth' or lines which seemed to indicate development, one of which was the move to a 'capacity for critical assessment', an achievement surely only found in any measure in the secondary years. The *stages* of this growth were not enumerated; there was in any case no evidence from research on which to base such an account.

Of 'those specialized yet centrally important uses of language which we refer to as literature', Whitehead claimed that there is a 'developmental sequence' which we work on instinctively, based on 'the kinds of experience which young readers can take, with benefit to themselves, from their reading of literature at different stages. The emphasis at first is psychological, 'with benefit to themselves', but there was a problem. How could such a paediatric pattern be 'reconciled with our wholly justifiable concern for quality and literary standards'? This dilemma (ignored by Dixon) between offering and steering, between reliance on the internal processes of growth and leadership from a mature standpoint, *is* difficult to resolve. However 'whichever conception of the teacher's role is adopted, it is certainly essential that his guidance should be disciplined by a sound and firm sense of values. He cannot pilot his pupil's taste towards "the good" in literature unless he has succeeded in arranging all the literary works he knows, both past and present in a hierarchical order of value – a hierarchy, moreover, which cannot be taken on trust from any "authority" and which needs to be continually reconstructed and modified in the light of fresh personal experience'.

This concern with 'values' in literature derived clearly from the parallel aim of 'the civilized human being' offering a direction and an end for growth, and guidelines for priorities in teaching. Some such criteria are necessary for the very understanding of the process (a process, to have any meaning at all, must have a product), but John Dixon, in his report, did not echo such preoccupations. No end was envisaged for development. We were encouraged to seek our model in the normal pattern of development, complex and varied as it may be. But 'normality' is to some extent a matter of choice; education is a matter of deliberate selection and emphasis. The Seminar had many voices speaking for some recognition of the importance of the culture. John Dixon did not represent these voices in his construction of the 'map' and so did not take account of the implications for teaching. Only twice in his book does he even acknowledge the existence of cultural influences from outside the classroom (he refers to 'the impoverished literature of the popular press' and later suggests that 'popular culture, depending so strongly on the media for mass-communication, is subject to continual change and some debilitation perhaps').

This examination of John Dixon's account of the Dartmouth Seminar has been a critical one, because of the implications of some of his central ideas. The task he was set was excruciatingly difficult and the measure of coherence he achieved is praiseworthy. Nothing new was introduced by the Seminar; nor did John Dixon introduce anything new himself other than the 'models'. His concern for learning was of a piece with the general criticisms of the excesses of 'subject-centred' teaching which were being made by all right-thinking teachers. There is no doubt that a coherent theory was being sought and Dixon's attempt (he expected it to be quickly superseded) was an impressive one. To criticize its faults is not to undermine its achievement.

The book presented a concerted effort to look at English from the child's end of education and explored in an exciting way the power of the active use of language to make meaning. It stressed throughout the importance of the child's involvement and interest. Dixon paid great attention to what was happening in the midst of learning, as against a ruinous attention in so many teachers to the finished product, the given. Finally, as I hope I have shown, Dixon very skilfully stitched together a view that spoke for and to many others at the time, an invitation to partnership in learning.

If that is true, a good deal of my criticism of Dixon must be accepted by others who failed at that time to develop a more comprehensive theory or to launch a forceful criticism of the limitations of the one Dixon voiced. Dixon offered a public perspective that was not, in many areas, far divorced from the views of Whitehead, Thompson et al; indeed Dixon at that time would probably have felt that he was speaking for them as well as for others like Britton.

In considering the state of affairs in 1966 and subsequent developments. it is the limitations which stand out. Though Dixon provided a temporarily effective consensus he did not reconcile all, nor did he apparently feel any failure, either in himself, in the Dartmouth Seminar or in the prevailing thinking at the time. The book confidently gave teachers an authority in criticizing teacher-dominated education. It failed to give an adequate authority for the teacher to act, because it failed to recognize the contribution of the past; it failed to set the classroom in its cultural context; it used, I suggest, a deliberately value-free theory of language as if it could answer the inevitably value-ridden questions of education.

Where lay now the authority, the confidence, of the teacher in selecting books for children?

Where lay the guidance for the teacher whose pupils said they saw no point in reading or writing?

Where lay the authority for any expression of judgment on the part of the teacher except as purely arbitrary and subjective?

Where, indeed, lay the authority for any insistence or persistence?

These questions are difficult to answer at any time, but they are open to working answers. Indeed, they have to be, if any education is to take place. They are just as important as those parallel questions aimed at insensitive domineering teaching.

Dixon, Dartmouth and kindred voices gave healthy impetus to a look at pupil-choice; greater variety in books and methods of study; the impetus to integrate activities in a flow of activity and participation. Characteristically, John Dixon saw his book as part of a continuing process and invited criticism; his model would, in the further movement of the dialectic, be superseded.

Is a new model for education struggling to emerge, just at the point when we have spelt out for ourselves the fuller implications of a model based on personal growth? Very well. The limits of the present model *will* be reached, that is certain, and thus a new model will be needed to transcend its descriptive power – and in so doing to redirect our attention to life as it really is.

Chapter 3

After Dartmouth – unity without coherence

Dartmouth and Dixon may have given a new emphasis to some approaches to English; they did not transform the scene. The implications of the underlying theory were only worked out gradually as it gained popularity. All the while there were critical voices, as well as influences quite different to John Dixon, at work in the field. In looking at the period after *Growth through English* only the main threads will be followed. These main threads will be, for clarity, separated, though in fact they merge and intertwine in the thinking of the time in a complex way. Nor will I follow the infinite variations on these general themes. However, I hope that with those qualifications, my picture will be a truthful and enlightening one.

Themes and Integration

One of the commonplaces of the new attitude to English teaching was the interrelatedness of all the ways of using language. This was partly in reaction against a cellular division of the subject into lessons; more importantly it was part of the energetic search for a unifying theory. The contributions of Denys Thompson and Frank Whitehead to this theory of the unity of English have been examined already; the ambiguity of the language used, especially 'central', was evidence of unresolved complications. The unity of classroom activities was strongly supported by John Dixon in *Growth through English*. He wrote 'If in the course of reading some poems with a class the teacher sees possibilities for acting or if in the accompanying talk pupils are so seized with the topic that they want to write, then a unitary approach permits the flow from a prepared activity to one relatively unforeseen. . . . What unifies such varied classroom activities is the theme or aspect of human experience on which work centres.'[48]

Such movements had been envisaged by the Dartmouth participants, without apparent dissent and it is noteworthy that Frank Whitehead quoted the above words of Dixon with apparent approval[49] and continued: 'our attention will be focused not on the work of literature as a thing-in-itself . . . but rather upon its capacity for interaction with the individual pupil, its relevance to his present emotional and intellectual needs . . .'

This fluidity, in which literature was to play its part, had a particular fairly predictable possibility, which was that literature might be used as the jumping off point, to stimulate discussion, to provide an idea for drama, to serve as a document on which to cut the teeth of social awareness, abuses which the Bullock Committee were to observe on their visits to schools in the early seventies. It would require a very strong appreciation of literature's own demands to resist the temptation to merge literature into a general 'unity', whether that dictated by the 'needs' of a particular pupil or the organization of the English curriculum into 'themes' of general importance.

In the late sixties, it was the role of 'themes' which came to dominate, stimulated particularly by the work of Anthony Adams and Geoffrey Summerfield, both participants at Dartmouth. Summerfield's main contribution was made, indeed, before that conference with his book *Topics in English*.[50] Here a number of themes, or 'topics' were offered – Predators, Heights, Old Age, Hunting and so on. The term was carefully defined as 'a given range of activities such as various forms of reading and writing, which are *unified* by a particular topic or theme' (my italics) and literature was to play a central role.

'It is ill-advised to use a poem or a short story invariably as a springboard for the pupil's own writing: we should be prepared to let literature *be*, rather than reduce it to the subsidiary role of stimulus . . . Literature is, I believe, the most important part of any English scheme of work . . .'

In the detail of the topics there were lists of activities ranging from individual reading to discussion to writing both 'expressive' and impersonal, by means of which pupils 'explore' an area of important experience. The choice of reading was often odd, frequently very demanding; the range of activities was long and disparate but little interconnected; the implication was that the unity was in the 'meaning' derived by the particular pupil. This is a point of some significance in subsequent developments in 'theme work'. The difficulty that has emerged in experience with this kind of teaching is to weld together effectively the various elements without forcing them into distorting shapes.

Anthony Adams placed his use of themes within the context of teaching as a team. The major and distinctive emphasis of his book (*Team Teaching and the Teaching of English*[51]), was organizational, presenting a way of working in an English department which provided a sense of collaborative direction. Adams was no more hostile to literature than

Summerfield; his confessed centre was literature and reading. Again, like Summerfield, his suggested literature was demanding; they both demonstrated the search for material outside the traditional limits. As an example of a theme we might take one on 'Landscapes' (Adams' term was 'a project') for the whole of the third year. Within this came Lawrence's *Nottingham and the Mining Countryside*; Wilfred Owen ('Landscape of War'); Sassoon's *Memoirs of a Fox-hunting Man*; A. G. Street's *Farmer's Glory*; Robert Frost. Under 'Localities and Customs' came *Lark Rise to Candleford, Cider with Rosie* and the writing of Hardy, Bennett, Lawrence, Barnes.

These schemes were very ambitious and very influential; they did, for a time, convey a sense of the unity of English. But the growing stress on learning inevitably led to looking at the receiving end. Certainly the pupil was encouraged to put together his own 'package', through which would emerge his own meaning. In the hands of some teachers, this might mean providing stimulating injections from time to time in the hope that some connexions would be made inside the child. Where, though, was the source of the confidence that this was so? Instead of confidence there emerged in time a feeling of dissatisfaction with the vagueness of it all. The coherence could not be taken on trust.

A further source of dissatisfaction with the approach was the way literature came to be used. In spite of the caveats of Geoffrey Summerfield, literature was increasingly plundered for material to fit the theme. Thus work of low quality would be included because of relevance to the theme. On the other hand a good book would be emasculated by the subjugation of what it uniquely had to say to the theme.[52] This latter danger was already apparent in the work of Summerfield and Adams. How could, for example, the unique quality of *Lark Rise to Candleford* fail to be destroyed by its use for 'Localities and Customs'? Literature had become social document, grist to a very extrinsic mill and the flood of books of material for themes which poured from publishers ransacked print for any relevant material.

An example of the way themes could become overpowering organizing forces came in an article in 1969 when adolescence was seen as the theme of Townsend's *Hallersage Sound* and the 'theme' of illegitimate pregnancy was seen to be sensibly handled by Kamm's *The Young Mother*.[53] The search for relevant material had come to that: which is not to say that books cannot be said to have themes, nor that books and authors may not be usefully contrasted by the way they approach some archetypal human experiences. Only that it must be done with care, arising out of respectful reading and attention to the complexity of what was written.

A parallel movement to create new unities can be seen in the attempts to integrate subjects in the curriculum. Are not the various subjects artificially separated while knowledge and learning are whole? If so, why are not the subjects, say, English, History, Geography, Religious Education and Social Studies united in an embrace called 'Humanities'. This persuasive case had great influence and English, with its recent inclination to extend the boundaries and break out of socially-created limits, has played a major part in the extension of 'integrated studies', 'interdisciplinary enquiry' and 'autonomous learning'. (The Schools Council Humanities Project is probably the best-known national example.) Literature again was subsumed as 'evidence' of 'problems', 'human issues' and so on.

It is doubtful whether this particular seam is yet played out, but it does contain the same fundamental problem as themework, without a solution to which the venture is doomed to failure and disappointment.

It is interesting that Anthony Adams has been sceptical about some of the schemes of humanities that have emerged, especially their arbitrary basis. 'The question of *what* we are trying to teach in the name of humanities remains . . . fundamental, and until that has been explored there is little point in a discussion of *how* it is to be taught.' And again 'Are there some things that ought to be included in the curriculum by design and not be left simply to chance or to special interests which may or may not arise?'[54]

If the various elements to be integrated are valuable it is because of what they uniquely are and how they have been approached before (somewhere at least). To import them without their concomitant distinctive demands is to include something very different. Thus literature included for its value as literature but treated as social evidence is not at all the same thing. The unique distinction of literature is *completely* lost in the process. On this has foundered most integration to date.

The criticisms of this kind of integration grew louder in the early seventies. Thus David Lindley wrote: 'an application of literature that ignores the intention behind, and the complexity of, the work in question, is an abuse'.[55] This was a very spirited attack, both general in the defence of a distinct subject ('the nature of any integrated humanities course is inevitably such that the purpose of English teaching can only be thwarted by involvement in it') and particular, on behalf of a distinctive contribution from literature. 'Literature worth reading will burst open any thematic course, whether of the integrated humanities or *Topics in English* variety.'

Brian Hollingworth, in the same edition, connected this same distorting integration with the urge to please, the search for 'relevance'. 'One of the most disturbing things about modern education is that what we teach and how we teach it seems very much determined by our culture's obsession with the consumer, and with the consumer's response and satisfaction'[56] and asserted, in contradistinction to this, 'the English teacher's concern must be in ensuring sympathy with the original intention, concern with the medium of execution, the poem as composed, rather than encouraging the pupil to use it for his own psychological or social ends'. The danger if literature were used in themes would be the same as in the concern for relevance. Hollingworth quoted George Watson: 'The demand for relevance to the modern condition amounts to a demand that the student should be confirmed in the existing values of his own civilization, and that he should never be offered the possibility of adopting another.'

The difference with themes is of course that the material, selected by the teacher and truncated to fit the theme, conveys the *teacher's* values. The teacher becomes a block on the plurality of voices instead of offering real choice. What is needed is, to return to the starting point, a unified theory of English which retains the unique qualities of reading, writing, speaking, drama, etc., safeguarding what they do best. A unity of uniformity does a violence in which nothing is what it best is. Because the unity sought by teachers did not sufficiently account for the *differences* between the elements, it was possible to pretend, at least for a time, that they were all the same, with sad consequences. Nor did the language model of James Britton construct any better account of the differences. Was this what David Lindley meant when he wrote 'In so far as it looks for "structures" of feeling and experience, seeks (paradoxically) to merge and classify, and accepts the trivial resemblances of the letter instead of the essential ones of spirit, then English succumbs, not only to an aimless march of philistines, but to a wider process that drifts towards nullifying the very word "value".'

Chapter 4

English as language – the touch of linguistics

Language . . . is the indispensable mechanism of human life – of life such as ours that is moulded, guided, enriched, and made possible by the accumulation of the past experience of members of our own species.

S. I. Hayakawa.

It would be to take a narrow, blinding view to pretend that developments in English teaching theory are always self-generated. Indeed, since English concerns itself with some variety of matter and has had a tendency to expand and engulf larger and larger areas, it might be truer to say that English teaching is inevitably bound to reflect thinking at large, outside the subject boundary, in more immediate ways than most school subjects. Such certainly has been its style in the period under consideration, with a good deal of impact from the spheres of sociology and politics, the psychological sciences, and, more predictably, from the formal study of language which has developed under the name of 'linguistics'.

There already existed in 1965 some general agreement that a wider range of language uses than the literary should be the concern of the English teacher, particularly in writing. Even more so if oral language were considered important. The general drift, in fact, was towards a consideration of the way language is used in the business of living as a long continuum of many different modes. Language, as a basic ingredient of our living, needed to be considered very seriously; it was what made us human.

However, to enter a caveat to this eminently reasonable view, what is meant by 'language' may vary a great deal from writer to writer and it is important not to allow a confusion of terms. What Frank Whitehead and Denys Thompson meant by language[57] included the idea of necessary value-judgements about the ways in which language was used in sensitive or insensitive ways, for noble or shabby purposes. There was indeed a vital critical element there. In this respect some uses of language are more worthy of consideration and use; the best kinds of language support a civilized existence.

On the other hand those who would look at language scientifically – 'as it really is' – and call their study linguistics point out that the

50

literary-critical frame of mind pays inadequate attention to a whole range of language uses which are worthy of consideration because of the wonderful complexities that are revealed. By *suspending* judgement, a breathtaking discovery of the subtleties of language in every situation is possible.

Such an interest in language among English teachers was reinforced by the work and publications of the *Nuffield Programme in Linguistics and English Teaching* led by Professor M. A. K. Halliday, which sought to consider what part linguistics could play in the teaching of English.

A central concept of the approach to language taken by the programme team, and derived from Firth (who had taught Halliday), was that language is infinitely adjustable to the particular subtle fluctuations of the situation. Thus they were interested in a very wide range of uses. Indeed it might be said that this wonderful variety provided one of the two important organizing principles; the other was the functional belief that ability to use the *variety* of language was a basic element in competent living. Thus 'a high proportion of educational failure is in fact linguistic failure';[58] a conclusion drawn from the work of Basil Bernstein and sharing the assumption that educational failure usually means loss of life-chances.

The project was launched in 1964 but it is likely that its major early influence was on a few influential figures, rather than on teachers at large. The first notice given at large was probably in the chapter written by Halliday for *Talking and Writing*, a collection of papers edited by James Britton.

The collocation of Britton and Halliday seems significant, since in spite of their differences they have sought to expound a *language* theory of English teaching.[59] Halliday called his chapter 'Linguistics and the teaching of English', mirroring closely the title of the project. He wrote 'There is probably no subject in the curriculum whose aims are so often formulated as are those of English language; yet they remain by and large ill-defined, controversial and obscure'. He then mounted what seems now to be a very cavalier claim that 'teaching the English language is a highly specialized task . . . and only the professionally trained English language teacher can perform it'. One wonders at the contribution of parents. He went on, 'If it is left in the hands of amateurs – and the English literature specialist who has no linguistic training is almost as much an amateur in this context as is the scientist or mathematician – we can expect the result to be a nation of inarticulates.' The equation of *language* experts with *linguistics* experts is gratuitous; the claim that articulacy is the result of specialist teaching is naïvely inflated; the general impression is one of large claims being made to justify a junior discipline. The article by Halliday was, it seems, an attempt to lay claims to territory held in the wrong hands, an attempt laid bare by his remark that 'The English teacher . . . if he is regarded as having any responsibility for his pupils' effective mastery of the language, needs to know his underlying discipline in the same way as does any other teacher, to at least the same extent; and the relevant underlying discipline here is linguistics.' The disarming analogy of the first part is crushed by the enormity of the final bland claim.

Nor is this merely a matter of the knowledge a teacher would find helpful. What was being mounted here was based on a conception of what teaching English ought to be; literature was seen as having an inflated place in the accepted teaching and language as linguistics was required to play a larger part. That agreed, the need for linguistic training would be obvious.

However, although the claims were large, they still represented to a degree the interest in widening the conception of English towards one concerned with language as a whole. In 1968 the Programme produced papers on a number of subjects. Paper 1, written by Peter Doughty and already referred to, 'The relevance of linguistics for the teacher of English' covered the same ground as Halliday, but in more moderate style.

'The native language, written and spoken, in all its variety, is a major component of all that goes on in an English class, a fact so obvious that perhaps its very obviousness has led to its being perpetually overlooked. A linguistic approach to language may offer the best possibility of constructing a unifying framework for work in English.' That is, the unity of English may be found in language as linguistics.

Again 'The value teachers place upon the varieties of written English found in the literature that receives critical approval and the degree to which those varieties become the measure of language use as such, sometimes spoken as well as written language, tend to obscure the importance of all the other varieties of English that do not qualify as varieties of literary English. If we regard the language as a whole, then the language of literature employs only a small number of the available ways of organizing the language for successful expression'.

It must be agreed that if literature-centred teaching does concern itself only with the literary, if it does obscure other *important* varieties of English, then it is misguided and deserves Doughty's strictures. But is there any need for such exclusiveness? And is *inclusiveness* without its problems for the teacher? How does inclusiveness solve the problems of decision, priority, choice? Are value and power in language not to be considered important qualities? Are we to believe in fact that all kinds of language are equally valuable and equally powerful? Doughty assumes the equality of all forms of language and considered the foundations for a career in teaching in the following way: 'Almost certainly, his (the teacher new to the subject) basic studies will have been literary and they will not provide him with the tools he requires, because, first and foremost, his tasks are with language, language in all its complexity and variety and not merely the highly idiosyncratic form of literature.' The queries here attach to the 'all' and to the confidence with which literature is described as 'highly idiosyncratic'.

No teacher can be concerned with *all* language; education is concerned with potential, not just with what is. An area of study might be very unpopular but essential, well liked and barren. The question, in short, of value cannot be answered in such a way.

Doughty was not 'against' literature. He accepted throughout his paper the contribution of literature as a kind of language and accepted its place within the school subject. In Paper 5 'Linguistics and the teaching of literature' Doughty concerned himself with the effects of the domination of English by literary men. He saw the claim for the 'centrality of literature' (as evidenced for example in the *Use of English* journal) as derived mainly from the particular specialism absorbed by the teachers – the academic study of literature.

When he came to consider attitudes to linguistics Doughty offered the following: 'a reappraisal of work in English from a linguistic point of view is likely to lead to a shift in emphasis; any such shift of emphasis away from a literature-based English teaching however very much parallels a similar shift apparent in much recent discussion' and refers to Frank Whitehead and John Dixon as examples.

Doughty is at pains to clarify his position. 'The question at issue is not *whether* to use literature . . . an absurd question once formulated . . . but what part it should play, how best to use it, and what contribution linguistic studies could make at this stage.' And he accepts that 'the relationship between pupils' experience of literature, and their enhanced power to handle both spoken and written English, is too well attested by teachers' practical classroom experience to be lightly set aside'.

Doughty was not alone. Indeed, there was a good deal of similarity in the writings of a wide range of specialists on the subject of language. It seemed in the late sixties that agreement was strong between the *Use of English* contributors, linguisticians and, say, the London University Institute of Education Department of English. However it is clear now that such a feeling of agreement could only be temporary. For example the sight of linguistics in U.S. classrooms given to those who went to

Dartmouth had created a severe scepticism about the kind of things the Programme in Linguistics might produce.

Also in 1968, the *Use of English* published a paper by Neil Postman, an American, which began by attacking the grammarian's linguistics in use in American projects, but suggested 'the primary goal in language teaching is to help students increase their competence to use and understand language, *especially those styles, varieties and functions of language that most intimately affect their lives.*[60] (My italics.) These remarks seem now to offer a bridge between what Postman calls 'linguistics as the rigorous study of language situations' – that is, what the Programme in Linguistics was attempting to provide – and those who saw a need for an informing sense of value and judgment. He pointed out an important omission from a scientific approach. 'The English teacher does not have the same freedom as the linguist in choosing the language systems he wants to scrutinize. The linguist is free to choose that which is merely interesting to him. The English teacher is – or should be – governed by a sense of what is important for his students to think about.'

Postman, then, faces up to the question of 'What is important?' He offers no specific detail on the role of literature; he does see the study of literary works as 'the study of a language situation' thus attempting a very similar kind of unity to that proposed by Doughty and others.

It might have appeared at the time of the publication of *Growth through English* that the relationship of language and literature was a clear one. That the problem remained to be settled is made clear in looking at an article by W. H. Mittins on 'Modern views of English language'.[61]

He began by saying that 'the catalogue of unanswered basic questions is far too long for comfort'. In particular 'What are the relationships between language and literature?' has not been answered. 'Literature is partial in that though relevant (and most valuably so) to all pupils it is but one of a vast range of language activities. It is only literature against the background of the language as a whole.' Any unifying conception 'must be based in fact on a definition of "English" as broad as any piece of human behaviour that is clearly meaningful language, whether spoken or written'. This would appear to be seeking unity at the cost of shapelessness and is very reminiscent of the image of James Britton that English is the rest of the pastry after the other subject shapes have been cut out.[62] It is hard to see any organizing principle, any meaningful selection being possible except on idiosyncratic grounds. He echoed the remarks of Whitehead and others that 'On educational grounds we must welcome the insistence that no one language is better than another' – as one of the valuable contributions of linguistics.

Such all-inclusiveness and the rejection of any hierarchies of language present problems. One, the problem of the curriculum, has been referred to. The idea of 'equality' of languages was derived from the realization that dialects were as complex and subtle as any other ways of speaking, in which case any supposed superiority must be more to do with attitudes towards the speakers, such as their class or social status, rather than the ways of speaking themselves. There was no substantial merit in one pronunciation, one vocabulary, one standard of correctness.

However it would be obvious nonsense to say that all language does the same job just as well; there are obviously levels of efficiency, some expressions are better than others. It might also be agreed that if our world-view and our moral values are largely suspended in our language, then some developments of language are more admirable than others, some might convey an inhumanity to man. (Is the language of aggressive, reductive insult as *valuable* as that of rational consideration?)

What seems to have happened, in extending the idea of equal merit, was analysed by Raymond Wilson in an article in 1969. 'The popular claim that all languages and dialects are of equal merit, each in its own way, is not a factual statement, since a philosophical leap is taken by anyone who moves from the assertion that discrete language activities exist to the assertion that they exist equally in terms of merit.'[63] Such a leap was outside scientific discourse because it was concerned with *values*. Thus paradoxically such writers as Mittins can be seen to be making a statement requiring consideration of values *in order to reject the idea of value*. 'In the minds of many advocates of linguistics, facts about language are often muddled with social values in such a way as to make an important practical difference to what they teach.' This appears to describe W. H. Mittins and the host of writers in the sixties who accepted the 'equality of languages'. Raymond Wilson continued 'If it is a fact that there are many Englishes, it is no less a fact that we have not world enough and time to teach them all.' The problem of what to include in the curriculum and what to exclude has to be solved; all-inclusiveness is no help there. Wilson, Professor of Education at Reading University at that time, put his weight in a very different place to Mittins and Doughty. 'Perhaps the new media and changing social conditions do require us to give more attention than we have formerly given to non-literary usage; but we are in danger of surrendering values altogether if we follow those linguists who assert that literature is merely one of many Englishes.' He concluded with a comment very similar to one of Neil Postman's. 'We must recognize that not all Englishes are of equal value to the children and . . . we are forced to be selective in our teaching.'

This issue of values in deciding what should be seen to constitute the subject English was discussed widely in the late sixties, working out with some repetition the questions raised at Dartmouth and before. We have already seen that some articles written earlier were considered relevant to this discussion. In 1970, Frank Whitehead published in *Use of English* a modified version of a paper he first wrote for Dartmouth 'Continuity in English teaching'. It will be remembered from the discussion earlier of the Dartmouth proceedings that Whitehead offered a pattern for English based upon the natural development of a child, if well fostered, towards a civilized adult. In this pattern literature reading of some quality was to play a crucial role. Language, the mother-tongue, was welcomed into the subject whose role was 'to foster, improve and refine the individual's ability to use his mother-tongue – to use it fully, flexibly, effectively, sensitively, and to use it for all the varied purposes which one's native language must serve in a modern civilized community' – a comment which indicates a substantial agreement with writers like Peter Doughty. However he is nearer to Raymond Wilson and to 'the damned and despised literati' who Doughty and Halliday characterized as 'amateurs' when he refers to 'those specialized yet centrally important uses of language which we refer to as literature'. The ambiguities of 'central' have already been examined; it is nevertheless clear that a 'central' function is worlds away from 'the highly idiosyncratic form' of language which Doughty called literature.

Such a disagreement concerning the exact relationship of language and literature – central or peripheral – was at the heart of the continuing debate, which became at times, as we shall see, acrimonious.

To sum up, there were two fundamental items in the debate:

1. The relationship of literature to language.

2. The organizing principle, or judgment of value, in the notion of 'language'.

At the 1971 Conference of N.A.T.E., on the theme of 'Language across the curriculum', Fred Inglis spoke rumbustiously about the issues raised by a school book recently published by the Nuffield Programme in Linguistics and English Teaching. Called *Language in Use* the book sought to provide materials for classroom use.[64] The address remains a very important one, pressing some severe criticisms at all of those who want English to mean language, as developed by such diverse characters as Doughty, Halliday and Britton. Pinning an eye on the *Language in Use* team he wrote 'we now need a much more careful and thorough-going critique of the characteristically English kind of applied linguistics (tautologically known as "context of situation"), especially as applied to English-teaching, and to suggest some of its drastic practical and conceptual limitations' and urged a series of specific criticisms.

1. Doughty's understanding of teaching literature did not account for its intention to answer the questions 'What for? What ultimately for? What do men live by?'

2. Doughty failed to realize that 'What literature means as a specialist term – largely a matter of genre: poems, dramas, novels (dead for a docket) – is not what it means in our lives. . . . Our intention in the study of literature is to register and agree upon the relative significance of the experience rendered in the words.'

3. English teachers of literary background were not necessarily 'narrow', as Doughty had seemed to believe. They had in general attempted 'to find and stand up for a central, a truly human point of view. . . . These teachers have taught the privacy of the individual sensibility, the unflinching need to keep your private self your own and clear, spontaneous, intelligble, and full of life.'

4. *Language in Use* failed to include meaning and morality in any way comparable with that offered by those same teachers of English.

5. History is left out of account. *Language in Use* is 'atemporal'. 'The uses of literacy are a product of our history and to ignore the changes in that history is to commit a moral error.'

The first three criticisms concerned the failure to understand what liteature in education is really about. As such they could as well be laid at the door of John Dixon, whose account has already been examined. Inglis was insisting that there are vitally important uses of words in literature that must be given an audience; that the *meaning* to the person of what is read in literature is crucial in the construction of a meaningful existence, far outweighing any benefit to be gained by a study of language in *all* its uses. And that is not because reading in general is more vital than speaking or writing but because there are in existence particular items of *achieved* significance. The plays of Shakespeare, the peoms of Donne, Keats' letters, Berger's *A Fortunate Man*, the novels of Laura Ingalls Wilder are all in their different ways achievements of meaning which offer us something we might not come to ourselves. (Obviously what is accessible to a twelve-year-old or a seventeen-year-old must be considered – but even so what is *good enough* to matter at a particular stage of growth must be given serious thought.)

One of the essential signs of maturity is the ability to come to important writings from other times and to feel their weight. The central characteristic of literature, that which argues for its importance and without which it is empty, is *meaning*. As Inglis says of some great letters, 'They fill one's mind to the brim. They alter the mind. They are profound and civilized in all their details. They become a part of one's life.'

In terms of the demand for priorities made by Neil Postman and Raymond Wilson, Inglis was clearly pressing the claims of literature against those of language as linguistics. However, Peter Doughty's energetic defence was not long delayed. To some extent of course Inglis' criticisms had been personal. They had also been specifically directed at the *Language in Use* materials. The ebullience of Inglis had stung, and the first part of the reply was a restrained plea for tolerance, particularly as Doughty felt he was suggesting an *inclusive* view of English.

On the question of value, Doughty referred to the questions called the central ones by Inglis 'What for? What ultimately for? What do men live by?' However 'It seems to me that there is a different kind of question to ask before we are in a position to ask the question at all meaningfully. Not *what* do men live by, but *how* do they live at all. . . . It is significant that the questions ask what *do* men live by, not what *ought* they to live by, and asking what men *do* live by is surely not the same thing as asking what they *ought* to live by.'[65] He continued by describing the attitude to language taken by the Programme team. One major aim was 'the development of an awareness of "*how* we use language to live"'. But 'developing an awareness of how we use language to live is not at all the same thing as being able to talk about the structure and function of language in the explicit terms appropriate to its analytical and academic study'. Further the underlying theory of the *Language in Use* approach embodied a view of language which makes it impossible to evade its 'value-laden' nature. It argued that a major concern for the linguistic study of language must be the part played by language in 'the creation and maintenance of cultural values'. Thus 'the work arising out of the work of any unit [in *Language in Use*] has to involve questions of value, because the activity of using language necessarily involves in some sense or other "the function of value integration"'. He then put forward a theory of language which did, in different vocabulary, seem to be saying very much what Denys Thompson had been saying in the sixties, though without any parallel faith in the efficacy of literature. Language has two main aspects. It is firstly 'the means by which we make sense of our experience of the world' (that same 'experience' presumably that was the central matter of English as agreed at Dartmouth and beyond). Secondly 'language functions as a link in concerted human activity', that is as the nexus for social activity of every kind. Hence a particular language comes to be 'a complex inventory of all the ideas, interests and occupations that take up the attention of the community'. A third dimension to language is 'to see it as the major means by which cultural values are transmitted from one generation to the next'.

Certainly, though I would suggest literature plays a part in such transmission, I could not claim it does it alone. Such a claim would be absurd. There are obviously other modes of discourse (like rational discussion, the sermon, the television interview) which have a crucial bearing on the creation and retention of a way of civilized existence. So much would be accepted presumably by all teachers of English and would serve as an area of neutrality between the embattled advocates of literature or language.

Doughty had answered the criticisms levelled at language-centred English by Inglis (though he did not reply to the charges of failure to understand what teachers of literature were about). His answers were powerful and provided a rationale for those who wished to explore further his approach to English through examining 'language in use'. Indeed in many respects there were strong *general* similarities between Doughty and Inglis, a point made by Don Salter in 1973.[66] He supported Doughty in accusing Inglis of being divisive in an unnecessary way, since there was a good deal of common ground. His main contribution was to claim that, in actually using *Language in Use*, 'Questions of morality constantly present themselves . . .' and 'there are countless examples . . . where it is impossible to shut the moral implications of language off from its mechanical processes'. This seems to counter the main criticisms from Inglis, which in turn suggests that the study of language may be capable of doing some of the very things that Inglis claims for literature. If this were so then there would arise the question as to what is left for literature to do. Is there anything it can do better? In general what part in this wide language awareness might literature play? The question put that way is implying a contributory role for literature, not as the core to the subject.

Yet what was still missing was a criterion for finding these utterances that repay close attention. Literature was assertively put forward by Inglis because it existed as a body of *meaningful* language, an achieved way of handling personal, human experiences – thus suggesting a characterizing centrality in the subject which concerned itself with such experience. The issue was not whether there were not other aspects of language that will yield up insights about human behaviour and values, but whether any other body of expression is as potent and coherent. Another aspect was the possibility of children exploring in their own art-speech the very same kinds of human concerns as are to be found in literature.

Leslie Stratta, co-author with John Dixon of the text-book *Reflections* and editor of *English in Education* offered as his judgment in 1972[67] that 'the old triad of literature, written composition and formal grammar ... has been giving way to new concerns, resulting in an almost bewildering variety of experiences and activities offered as appropriate to the subject. Twenty years ago a teacher of English might have confidently asserted that his main concern was to introduce his pupils to literature. Today he might less confidently assert that his main concern is with the process of helping his pupils to develop their abilities in using language for a variety of needs and purposes.' Where exploration of human relationships was concerned 'there had been a tendency to move from exploring these relationships mainly through literature to exploring them by using a variety of methods and media in addition to literature'. It will be recalled that James Britton specified at Dartmouth that it was the nature of English and literature to concern itself with personal experience and relationships. Some change had indeed taken place, for the influence of Britton in the years since Dartmouth has certainly not been to promote the reading of literature.

In the attempt to widen the subject beyond what Leslie Stratta called 'the old triad', there did not seem to be any real gain in the unity of the subject, as he indeed implied in 'an almost bewildering variety'. Nor could this search for coherence be long satisfied by approaching the stuff of English as 'using language for a variety of needs and purposes'.

Which needs? Which purposes? How to decide? Was any *educational* purpose suitable or were there language uses more appropriately left to other disciplines? Was a large variety valuable for its own sake? The problems of criteria for inclusion, of coherent connection – selection, priority, value – remained, and could not be answered from within a neutral 'language' theory of English.

The Bullock Report, *A Language for Life*,[68] can be seen as a culmination of a search for a language rationale for English, alongside a belief in the unity of English. The committee expressed faith in 'the organic relationship between the various aspects of English' and 'the principle that reading, writing, talking and listening should be treated as a unity'.

The Report covered a lot of ground with a fair amount of good sense, being sceptical about large claims for this or that panacea for all our ills, but we should not expect too much from a committee of varying voices. We might look to get a *comprehensive* treatment of a subject – covering all the ground, drawing in all the voices. A committee (that renowned designer of camels) is not likely to achieve an internal coherence, and the Bullock Committee did not do so. Though it asserted the 'organic' nature of English, we can scour the report from cover to cover without finding the specific *interrelationships* between the various elements – such a report is not the place to find it. What the report did offer was some of the materials required for specifying such interrelationships – it did point out some of the misuses and abuses of reading and talk; and it did attempt to specify some of the distinctive qualities of writing and talk.

Thus on the subject of misuses of literature, the report described how during their visits to schools 'there were several occasions on which virtually no attention at all was given to the words on the page. "Have you had an experience like this?" is a tempting question after a first reading; but it becomes valuable only if the experience is then brought back to the text, and if there is a sharpening of response to the detail of the writing'.

On writing, the report pointed out that 'Written language has to take on a precision and complexity of linguistic structure that is not demanded of speech' whereas 'When children bring language to bear on a problem within a small group their talk is often tentative, discursive, inexplicit and uncertain of direction; the natural outcome of an encounter with unfamiliar ideas and material.'

These are valuable comments to have, but the report, in spite of its comprehensiveness, left us with original problems of *coherence*. The committee accepted, without criticism, the language model of James Britton, who was a member of the committee, and whose influential contribution to English teaching will be examined more fully in the next chapter.

Chapter 5

Alternative centres – the contribution of James Britton

No account of developments in English teaching over recent years would be complete without a look at the work of James Britton, who has been probably the single most influential figure of the time; as we have seen, John Dixon's underlying view of language and literature was Britton's. Britton not surprisingly has always valued the contribution of international co-operation, especially at Dartmouth. He has written 'The transatlantic dialogue, highlighted by Dartmouth and York (1971), has been an important source of new thinking about English teaching'.[69] This is clearly because, as has already been suggested, Britton feels that the directions taken have been the right ones. There is a sense of satisfaction in his Introduction to the third edition of John Dixon's book *Growth through English*, that looking back brings a sense of work well done. Apart from his personal influence, which has obviously been strong (he has had enthusiastic followers at the London University Institute of Education and in the Writing Projects), he has had greatest permanent impact through his thoroughgoing construction of a theory of the functions of language already in evidence at Dartmouth.

To recall his remarks there, Britton offered a very useful schema of language uses which facilitated the construction of a 'map' of the country. 'We all use language in both these ways, to get things done in the outer world and to manipulate the inner world'.[70]

These two uses were called, repectively, *participant* and *spectator* and were ascribed to the roles taken up by the user. The spectator role comprised a physical detachment from the event being contemplated which may be actual or imagined and the language employed in this role was characterized by a wider perspective. 'When we *speak* this language the nearest name I can give it is "gossip"; when we *write* it, it is literature.'

This connexion of gossip and literature was not new at the Dartmouth Conference. He had already offered it to the 1965 Conference of N.A.T.E., claiming D. H. Lawrence as the progenitor, with his linking of the novel with gossip. His other influence was D. W. Harding who in an article in Scrutiny had examined 'The role of the onlooker'.[71] Harding wrote 'It is in this detached, non-operative evaluation that the spectator's role most commonly consists'. He claimed some importance for 'gossip . . . through which the possibilities of experience – reported or imagined – may be communicated and *evaluated*'. (My italics.) And finally 'The playwright, the novelist, the song-writer and the film-producing team are all doing the same thing as the gossip, however innocent they may be of writing propagandist intentions'.

It was, you will remember, this idea of 'language in the role of spectator' that became the working definition of literature employed at Dartmouth and by John Dixon, allowing the inclusion in the definition of children's own writing, as well as expression through other media. Britton's theoretical construct provided a very powerful justification for that widening, even though it omits the question of *quality* of utterance completely; it was intended for a different purpose. In addition the vexed question of the unity or duality of 'language' and 'literature' was apparently answered by Britton's language schema. The distinction was 'time-honoured but dying', so that in the book *Talking and Writing* 'much will be found that comments upon those uses of languge we commonly call literature and attempts so to place them in a wider context of language activities that the distinction becomes more and more difficult to make, and more and more artificial when it is made'.[72]

The position taken by Britton in that book was very much akin to that of Doughty and Halliday (see Chapter 4). In so far as English as a subject is concerned, language is its matter; literature is a part only of its various uses and functions. Yet this is a shift since Dartmouth.

> I suggest that the area in which language operates in English lessons is that of personal experience, in other words, relations with other people, the identity of the individual – the relation between the ego and the environment.
>
> We English teachers operate by what I call the spectator role, not the participant role. In other words we use literature. After all the themes of literature are the human themes.[73]

There Britton seemed to be still centring on literature as the matter for English, as though the implications of his 'language in the role of spectator' had not yet struck home. Perhaps it was the Seminar's discussions which did that work.

In evaluating Britton's theories of language it is important to realize that underlying them was a conception of how language works in the construction of a person's world-view, which is both unique and similar to that of others. 'We use language as a means of organizing a represen-tation of the world – each for himself – and that the representation so created constitutes the world we operate in'.[74] His basis is identical to that claimed by Peter Doughty drawing on 'George Kelly's theory of personal construct'. This construction is a life-long process and 'in many kinds of spoken and written communication – including those kinds that we particularly value in English lessons – we shape language most effectively at the point of utterance'. This is an active, creative effort which requires active language – thus talking and writing are particularly valuable here. The receptive uses – reading and listening – might seem less helpful. In the excitement promoted by this new realization, quite understandable in the light of its fertility and the resultant revelations, it was easy to forget that we gain a good deal of our sense of value, significance and meaning from others. Britton accepted this – 'To a very large degree, in any society, we build in common a common world picture.' Yet the novel idea of a personal unique construction, particularly alongside a child-centred pedagogy, was too dynamic for the sense of balance. Perhaps even some imbalance was necessary for the new areas to be given proper consideration. Be that as it may, the full contribution of literature, received achievement, was not as fully endorsed, its use not so fully encouraged. Was it assumed that literature was sufficiently entrenched to look after itself?

Britton's fullest expression came in his book *Language and Learning*. The title indicates the orientation. The learning of interest to Britton is a particular kind. The outlines of his view of the 'personal construction of a world picture' have been given. In this he was much influenced by an American psychologist, George Kelly, who 'suggests that all men behave in what is essentially the way a scientist behaves'.[75] That was according to Britton 'to formulate hypotheses, or to make predictions about the way things are, and then to put these to the test of what actually happens, and reframe his hypotheses in the light of what does happen'. Now this view of how a scientist operates has largely been discredited, by such writers as Michael Polanyi, on two main grounds. Firstly it fails to take full account of intuition, the leap of imagination. Secondly it omits the contribution of the culture through which we can adopt very effective hypotheses already well established.

What Britton and Kelly find attractive is the personal learner as romantic isolate. True, Britton looks to Martin Buber for the cultural dimension. 'Experience comes to man "as I" but it is experience "as we" that he builds into the common world in which he lives.' Britton glosses this with 'We each build our own representation of the world, but we greatly affect each other's representation, so that much of what we build is built in common.' But at what point do we have a view of experience that is *wholly* personal – 'as I'? Do we not from the very first experience in a context given by others? Is not our individuality to a very important extent gained by the submission to a rich culture, rich in choice that is? What is omitted is the contribution of the past.

My criticism should not be seen as an attempt to supplant the *personal* character of learning; rather to assert the dual, reciprocating nature of knowing – it is *both* personal *and* common, both are suffused in the process of experiencing, as a human being among other humans. In Britton's work the cultural dimension is being under-rated to a debilitating extent, and what would follow is a tendency, in a written culture, to undervalue literature. Of course we may read and take what we will for our personal construct. Compare John Dixon's 'The *writing* that springs from literature takes us in two directions; outwards into our own shaping of experience, tapped and activated by our reading and that is the usual direction – or in towards the writer's experience, sifting and savouring the thing for itself – and that is rarer'. But the too markedly personal account will not encourage the sense of obligation, of gifts offered by another to be remade and taken with effort. The taking would have to be personal but it also needs to be submissive, *responsive*.

Britton, drawing on Ernst Cassirer and Susanne Langer, sees language as a means of representing in symbolic form the experiences before us. 'The primary task for speech is to symbolize reality; we symbolize reality in order to handle it once we see man as creating a representation of his world so that he may operate in it, another order of activity is also open to him: he may operate directly on the representation itself.'

Such a function is not limited to speech, of course. Writing does the same and so does literature; indeed all the arts do just that, though it would be foolish to pretend that the only symbolic orders in a developed culture are artistic. Even so it would appear to be one of the central functions of art in general to offer a representation on which we may ponder, which we may evaluate, as if it might be reality, though we know it is not. This is an aspect partly appreciated by Britton when he equates 'literature' with 'language in the role of the spectator' and says: 'We become experienced people as a result of the fusion of other people's experiences with our own', implying that literature is 'virtual experience', and making a needed contribution.

There can be no doubt, indeed, from a reading of Chapter 3 of *Language and Learning* – 'Participant and Spectator' – that James Britton takes literature seriously as a factor in growing maturity. The case is developed with some vigour in the total exposition. However, there are a number of aspects of particular significance in accounting for his influence in a *lessening* interest in literature.

Firstly, 'language in the role of the spectator' is deliberately a neutral term. As he wrote: 'it is helpful to have a way of defining literature which refers to the sort of thing *it is* rather than one which brings in the judgement as to how good it is of its kind. It is not that I feel the question "how good is it?" is not a highly important question, but I think it should come *after* and not instead of the question "what is it?"' However Britton is really not interested in the 'highly important question', for nowhere in the book does he consider it. He is concerned largely with categorizing ('What is it?') and seeing what the various kinds of language *do*. There is nothing culpable in such an interest though it must be repeated that *education* must be concerned with questions of choice, criteria and quality. There has been some gain in seeing the kind of writing done by children as in important ways similar to that of a mature writer, but . . . which brings us to a second feature of the theory.

The studious avoidance of value-judgements in the language model constructed by Britton has been at the expense of ignoring important differences. Quality ('how good it is of its kind') is absolutely central in determining the matter of English studies. If maturity is the aim, all examples within a category of writing are not equally valuable – indeed some will be useless or even damaging. The particular model proposed by Britton is of no help in making decisions. Indeed, anyone who is convinced of the rightness of Britton's theory as an account of language as a whole (for that is what it purports to be) might be also convinced that there is no important distinction to be drawn between the writings of the immature and the mature. If so, then what John Dixon called 'the literature of the classroom' – the children's own writing – simply because it is more accessible, might be more attractive than books, which are usually much more demanding of time and effort.

Thirdly, what James Britton constructed purported to be a theory of language in education, of which literature was only one kind. As such it very much parallels the theories of Halliday and Doughty in their Programme in Linguistics Project.[76] An important difference between them is that Britton does give some account of the function of literature (whereas Halliday and Doughty vary between a vague assumption of value and a suspicion that literature might well be rested without great loss). Even so, the influence of Britton would be towards equality *inter pares*. The implications of his theory lead naturally, it would seem, into a concern for the development of a range of 'languages' by pupils. Indeed Britton has had a great influence on the 'Language across the curriculum' movement, which seeks to improve the ways language of more impersonal kinds is used in schools. He has also had a seminal influence on Douglas Barnes, whose interest has moved more and more towards the language of 'content' subjects and away from English altogether.[77]

As a 'language-studies' man, Britton, too, came in for some criticisms from Fred Inglis. Inglis believed that *Language and Learning* would 'be a critical force in legitimating language study of many different kinds'.[78] The book was accused of emptying language of morality and of its history. It was in reference to Britton that he catalogued a number of great letters of the past as 'great poems'. He continued: 'They fill one's mind to the brim. They alter the mind. They are profound and civilized in all their details. They become a part of one's life. But Britton cannot tell us what to do with such experiences'.

Inglis leads us to the conclusion that such a theory of language as Britton's *cannot* account for the 'important question' of 'how good is it?' This leads in turn to wondering how such an important omission might have originated. Inglis' explanation is characteristically apocalyptic and political but points to some interesting possibilities. 'Britton gives us the liturgy of our modern and educational neo-liberalism: the nervous decency, the generosity and helplessness, the anxious rejection of moral decision and diagnosis, the forlorn hope that "All shall be well and all manner of things shall be well".'

Britton, and others under his influence, such as Douglas Barnes, do seem to believe that children will arrive at maturity by their own efforts, creating an adequate world-picture out of the material that comes their way by active talk and writing. It is a faith fundamental to the progressive ethic, shown in the child-centred approach of the British team at Dartmouth and in the 'progressive cutting-edge' of English teaching in the 1960s. Britton's theory is a direct offshoot of the thinking of that time, not a wholly new growth. His 'learning' is at the centre of his thinking, just as the British team at Dartmouth were trying to insist that the only criterion for good teaching was effective learning and that it was the learning end of the process which should receive our attention.

Britton's later formulation could not have been written in 1966 (some of the social changes had been dramatic) but when asked to write in 1973 a paper on 'How we got here' he said: 'We have learnt from bitter experience that there is in the long run no means of enforcing learning. We have come to recognize that the most precious means to a child's progress in learning is his own acknowledged responsibility for it; and, complementary to that, that we have no diviner's rights or powers by which we could so predict the society he will live in that we dare take on that responsibility ourselves.'[79]

Here, in the doubts about the contribution of the teacher, is an echo of the loss of nerve so in evidence among English teachers in the seventies. Thus also, the 'anxious rejection of moral decision and diagnosis' (claimed by Inglis) and the rationalist's new world. Britton's achievement has been great; but at very great cost.

Chapter 6

New Priorities – the search for social welfare

An attitude to teaching which stresses uniqueness and individuality is likely to extend itself into wider social concern, since no firm lines can be drawn between cases for educational/professional sympathy and a concern for social deprivation and injustice. The two tend to go hand in hand as part of a whole, the one confirming the other. Thus a concern for the individual child is increased by knowledge of poverty or home difficulties preventing that child from realizing his educational potential. When the difficulties are found to lie within the particular school system, the concern will impel a radical criticism. When the difficulties are found to lie in the social system without, then social and political questions become relevant to education. Already, at Dartmouth, the questions of school organization were being thrashed out as crucial to the subject English – a tripartite or a comprehensive system, streaming or mixed ability. It was felt that separation led to unequal treatment and hence injustice. The central drive here was egalitarian, fired by the influential findings of the fifties and sixties in the fields of sociology and socio-linguistics,[80] available in the writings of A. H. Halsey and Jean Floud, Brian Jackson and Denis Marsden, J. W. B. Douglas, Basil Bernstein and Denis Lawton, and in the Newsom Report.

The hopes for the grammar/technical/modern school system of the 1944 Act had been great; it was felt that equal opportunity was there. Such hopes were increasingly confounded as evidence accumulated that working-class children were not reaching their potential in the grammar school. They were leaving as soon as possible and under-achieving. A. H. Halsey and Jean Floud in *Social Class and Educational Opportunities*[81] showed that there was undoubtedly a class bias in educational success. The grammar school was not working as the mechanism of opportunity. J. W. B. Douglas in *The Home and the School*[82] showed that the bias began to work at the very earliest levels of education; that in fact the education system seemed quite dramatically to weed out the working-class children. To succeed equally the working-class child had to have *greater* ability. The causes of this unfortunate effect were complex but could be divided into two main categories: (i) the nature of the home and (ii) the particular character of the education offered. Broadly speaking there was a mismatch between the two. Jackson and Marsden[83] showed in some detail the pressures on the working-class child at grammar school to reject either the ways of his home or his education.

When the larger population was considered it was increasingly felt that the majority of working-class children received a very unsuccessful education. The Newsom Report *Half our Future*[84] attempted to consider what an appropriate education would look like for the majority of the school population, a task which was felt to be increasingly urgent – there was a crisis of confidence in the secondary modern school that what was being provided was not appropriate – not 'relevant' – to the needs of the children and society at large. In effect, there were grounds for a sense of injustice on behalf of children.

The work of Basil Bernstein into the role of language in educational failure was particularly influential (interestingly enough none of his work seeks to demonstrate factors in *success*). Over a number of years, Bernstein evolved the theory that there were two kinds of language – two 'codes' – which he called 'elaborated' and 'restricted'. It was the nature of the first that it was 'context-free' – ie, could handle hypotheses, the future, features absent from view – whereas the 'restricted' code was limited to what was present in the context. The main claim of Bernstein was that to a significant extent working-class upbringing did not develop the 'elaborated code' whereas middle-class upbringing fostered both codes. The assumption throughout was that secondary education in particular was dependent on competence in the elaborated code. Bernstein's work has been very influential in many areas giving impetus to one research project after another. Perhaps the most recent is that of Joan Tough at Leeds who seeks, on Bernstein's hypothetical framework, to find ways of *teaching* the elaborated code to pre-school children. Probably the writings of an ex-teacher of English, Denis Lawton, did most to disseminate Bernstein's ideas to the teachers at large.[85] In a work which to an extent was a critique of Bernstein's work he offered confirmatory evidence 'to support the view that inadequacy of linguistic range and control is a very important factor in underachievement and that linguistic inadequacy is a cumulative deficit'. He went further however; 'these linguistic difficulties relate to wider questions of motivation and culture (not simply language)'.

A. H. Halsey showed one way forward as Director of the Educational Priority Project which insisted that 'Educational provision alone cannot solve even the problem of educational priority, if only because in this sphere there are *no* purely educational problems.'[86] What the Project supported was 'positive discrimination' in terms of finance for schools with particular difficulties, together with 'an alternative curriculum realistically related to the Educational Priority Area environment' and the use of the school as focal point for the life of the surrounding community, responding to the needs of the community rather than imposing a pre-conceived notion of the good. 'Not only must parents understand schools, schools must also understand the families and environments in which the children live. . . . Only if education in the schools is relevant to the children's direct experience will it engage their attention and interest.'

The relevance of this last comment to the direction being taken concurrently by English teaching is obvious. The use of novels about working-class life for working-class children was very much confirmed. On the other hand, it might seem that if direct experience is what matters then literature of any kind is secondary.

The danger of such courses would be that the child might become trapped in a schooling which mirrors his world and does not show him other possibilities. Books do help us to make sense of our world but they also show us alternatives to which we may turn. An exclusive concern for the child's class and social environment cannot fail to diminish the child, who is *always* far more complex and individual.

If we return to the world of English teaching and seek signs of thinking similar to or influenced by these social scientists, there seem to be a number of particularly important ones, though one kind of influence would not show itself much in the writings about English teaching at all. That is, when the particular concerns of English as a subject seemed no longer important at all in the face of the more desperate problems. Many English teachers have come to that in inner-city schools.

An early sign of the influence of social scientists was the espousal of the progressive front of English teaching to the cause of comprehensive schools and mixed ability groupings, eg Tony Adams: 'the movement towards comprehensive schools will continue and the pressures in the future will be towards unstreamed comprehensive schools with mixed ability groupings for most subjects. My own view is that this is a highly desirable thing in any case from the point of view of a teacher of English.'[87] The Dartmouth Seminar had supported such developments.

However the new system was felt to demand rethinking. Esmor Jones wrote: 'The comprehensive situation was, for us, an entirely new one and required us to go back to first principles, to a rethinking of our whole attitude towards the teaching of English.'[88]

Such an opportunity was one to be welcomed especially as it allowed the whole school population to be considered for a genuine education, even if there were difficulties about implementing such a plan.

Another sign was the interest in the political and social implications of particular approaches to English. This aspect was exemplified by Commission 7 at the 1973 Conference of N.A.T.E., which stressed just these aspects. Later, in Spring 1975, a whole issue of *English in Education* was devoted to 'English and the social context' with articles such as 'The political element in English literature' and 'Marking as a mechanism of social control'.

There was also a developing concern to implement improvements in the education of the failing working-class. For example, the remedial classes in schools are made up largely of working-class children, though in considering the 'Language of Failure' the N.A.T.E. special Anglo-American seminar in Walsall (1968) was not often thinking primarily of class matters. Tony Adams wrote 'The problem of the disadvantaged is above all a human problem: the language of failure is the failure of us as teachers to deal at all adequately with the problems our pupils present us with.'[89] And Esmor Jones added 'It was no surprise [at the seminar] that the most crucial factor in teaching the disadvantaged was to be relevancy. (sic) The teacher cannot increase the option, linguistically speaking, unless he starts where the child is. Therefore teaching must start from the experiences of the children. As classroom talk encourages verbalization of these experiences, there should also be a planned introduction to new experience, both first-hand and vicarious through literature.'[90] Notice that Jones, a student at Leavis' college and a literature enthusiast, saw no irrelevance in literature for even the most disadvantaged, but what about those less enthusiastic in their support? Perhaps they might never arrive at the point when literature seemed 'relevant'.

Where, in a more 'open', less authoritarian society, there was a growing disaffection among the school population at large, it was felt that 'relevance' was a criterion to be employed at all levels. Especially was this so in thinking about raising the school-leaving age.

The raising of the school-leaving age, as recommended by the Newsom and Crowther reports, raising in its turn, for new consideration, a new group in the school population – the 'Newsom children', who would have preferred to leave and who had already been disaffected in their fourth or even third year in the school. This group posed a severe challenge to the normal assumptions of schools – more of the same was clearly a recipe for failure with those for whom it was a failure already. It was from this failure that much of the power of the concept of 'relevance' was derived. School was a failure because it was not 'relevant' to the lives the children were living or were about to live when they left school. Schooling was not about the 'real' world as the children experienced it.

This event (raising the school-leaving age) led to an acceptance of the theory of relevance as a survival measure. It seemed to offer a way towards a bearable solution. Because the problem loomed so large and because it was in the event impossible to isolate the reluctant pupils from the whole new compulsory school population, the influence of this R.O.S.L.A. thinking was such that it moved to the centre of the theory of English teaching, supporting the use of fiction and drama for socially relevant topics, and the move out quickly from the reading to a consideration of the 'real' world of social problems.

The problem was so enormous that, according to Fred Flower, 'it is not a question of discovering a new area of subject matter, a fresh stock of information as yet untouched and then devising a set of techniques for getting it across. We have to reconsider the purposes of education in relation to the actual pupils before us.'[91]

It might seem strange now that such a partial change in population should necessitate a thoroughgoing reconsideration. Rather it was that the actual sense of failure of schooling in so many cases led to a crisis in confidence and a search for new ways. R.O.S.L.A. itself can be said to have precipitated the rethink by the threat it posed to the structure of the schools. Failures could not be hived off, balanced against successes, any longer.

Some measure of the exasperation and failure sensed by many teachers faced by disaffected pupils can be gained from a reading of an article published in 1967, in which Michael Cullup berated the *Use of English* journal. None of the copies of the journal, he said, 'contains an article on the real situation inside a Secondary Modern School 'C' or 'D' stream classroom. However clever the spelling games, however bizarre the creative stimuli, however well-documented the experiences of getting children to write, however serious the reading-lists, they don't solve the worst problems – the problems of genuine confrontation.'[92]

Here was a problem being newly articulated – from the receiving end – and it seems rather amazing now, as if the education of a majority of the population had not been considered at all. Here was a plea to do more than child-minding, with a touch of desperation about it. It reads strikingly now, when it is commonly said that teaching is more difficult than it has ever been.

The 'reconsideration of the curriculum' was, then, in the direction of relevance. If we seek some more detailed clarification of the way the term was used we find the following:

A major contribution to educational retardation is social and intellectual deprivation. One of the more powerful antidotes is experience. Many of the successful experiments in secondary schools are looking for ways to help pupils digest the experience they already have and to offer them new experience which is felt to be relevant . . . They aim to start from a question the pupils consider interesting and to devise experiences which will suggest an answer. [93]

In such a schema reading would tend to be selected for its connexion with public, social problems – and for very good reasons. If the power-lessness of the deprived needs to be met in the community in which they live, one way of restoring power is by helping to articulate response to that community in 'political' terms. However what this means for literature is that it is *used* in the service of a greater cause. (At the worst it is used as propaganda without concern for any inherent quality.) The lines between literature and sociology are blurred, even unimportant. Thus, Michael Marland offered the scripts of a television 'cops and robbers' series as useful for either English or Social Studies in order 'to help classes towards an understanding of the social questions of today'. [94]

The final culmination of the increasing political bent is shown when the extrinsic aims come to override all other considerations; thus novels of middle-class life are rejected because of that (if they are well-written that is all the more reprehensible because they are more seductive); working-class writing is lauded for its own sake; literature must reflect 'the multicultural society in which we all live'. Such inverted judgments are those of a minority, to be sure, but they do, even at their extremes, have their breeding in the interplay of political sociology and English teaching.

A more moderate, articulate and central voice was that of Brian Hollingworth who in two articles for the *Use of English* developed a view of English teachers as political agents by nature and the new English as being particularly so orientated. In the first [95] he proposed to show that the pragmatic, tentative, individual style of the 'new English' was a kind of existentialism, aimed at the creation of an 'open' non-authoritarian society. He drew particularly on the comments of Basil Bernstein and Karl Popper to substantiate the claim, hoping to show that the English theorists were saying much the same thing. [96] The aims of English were seen to be to construct a new society and to this end 'A less exclusive approach to literature, a less intense and puritanical approach, an acceptance that literature is there as one of the good things of life and not *the* good thing, could help. In the open society we must not be afraid of multiplicity, nor of rejection, nor even of immaturity. Our pupils must be free to choose, and even to choose what we regard as immaturity.'

This critique of some approaches to English was continued in the later article [97] in which he claimed that 'the English teacher seeks to justify himself from within a cocoon woven by the arguments of literary theorists' so that he is 'unaware of possibilities which there are for providing a theoretical framework for native language teaching beyond the traditional limits of our literary-critical heritage'. He quoted Popper who asserted, even more strongly than did Peter Doughty, that the exclusive study of literature disqualifies the recipient for a place in a mature (i.e. open) society ('it often fails to educate him to intellectual honesty') but concluded that 'The point where literature becomes significant in modern society . . . is where it provides a sympathetic and intelligent analysis of the human problems which they, as individuals meet in establishing themselves within an uncertain world.' The overriding end was nevertheless political – 'English studies plainly have an important part to play in promoting the open society'. Which by its nature is unlike any society yet created.[98]

Conclusion

Enough has been said to show that the general influence of these sociological and political approaches has been towards seeing literature as either peripheral to the business of education or as making a contribution, with careful selection, to more important aims than those indigenous to the field of English teaching. Such a tendency need not be followed to the end. The characteristic may only tinge the teacher a little; it is the nature of English teaching at the present time to be a mixture of incompletely resolved influences, a collection of part-hogs, never the whole hog. However it is unlikely that any teacher is wholly uninfluenced, since teaching *always* has a political dimension.

The strength of the idea of 'relevance', a word now rather *passé*, was to encourage the attempt to adapt the curriculum to what the pupil brought with him, away from a too easy belief that it was the child's fault that he could not assimilate what was being offered. As such it was part of a search for materials and approaches which would work.

The weakness of the idea was that it had a simple view of the child behind it, understressing the power of a child's imagination in breaking the limits of his world. Paradoxically, a teacher responsive to the 'relevance' couched in pupils' reactions could find himself rejecting fiction as not relevant to the lives of the pupils because too often concerned with a foreign world, yet talking to those same children about TV programmes that were largely fanciful and wholly unreal.

There were, therefore, warning voices raised against some of the dangers inherent in this attempt to modify education for the sake of the working-class child. Surprising among them in the light of his remarks about pupils being free 'to choose what we regard as immaturity', was

Brian Hollingworth, who saw that the pupil could be confined within the values of his own community, denied choice and rendered more surely powerless by a lack of wider perspective.[99]

Even earlier, Sidney Bolt, for long an advocate of the value of literature in F.E. English courses, attacked the dominance of the search for 'relevance' as part of a critique of the influence of *Growth through English*. He described how the necessarily limited experience of the pupil might lead to a firm rejection of some experience described in fiction – that is, it would be felt by such a pupil to be irrelevant to his life. Bolt countered 'to object that this does not happen to people in experience as we know it is to make an irrelevant reference to our experience'.[100] One which, I might add, restricts our own growth for the wrong reasons, imprisoning us in a cocoon of ignorance.

Bolt was reasserting a view expressed at Dartmouth, by Barbara Hardy and others, that in reading an essential is to approach attentively, seeking what is there. A prior sense of the *limitations* of one's own experience is required, allied to a readiness to make use of one's own experience and forging the connexions possible as one proceeds.

Finally, David Shayer, in a survey of English teaching, pointed up another pitfall of the search for relevance – the abandoning of the writing of quality for the local, class voice (implying that good writing is in the end classless and for everybody). 'If "middle-class literature" is out and the prosaic "relevance" of Barstow and Braine are in, we have effected a very dubious exchange, to say the least.'[101]

The dubiousness, it ought to be said, would be at the expense of our pupils.

Chapter 7

Old wine, old bottles?

Literature is language charged with meaning. . . . Great literature is simply language charged with meaning to the utmost possible degree.

Ezra Pound

So far I have examined those tendencies which would lead to a reduced, even peripheral role for literature. However, there was a great deal of thinking which did not go along with this general drift. Much, on the contrary, was concerned to argue the vital importance of literature, though in ways which often showed a rethinking in the light of the concern for the child's needs and a changing social environment. One case of such rethinking was really a continuation of moves going back a long way.

Against a feeling that the canon of literature which had ossified in the grammar school curriculum was in need of re-examination, English teachers in the fifties and sixties were attempting to extend the range of reading while still retaining some quality. Such a re-examination was supported by a strong belief that the children should enjoy the books they read and feel that they spoke directly to them at their age, not when they recalled them as mature adults. Width of choice was a necessary component, as was accessibility, both physical (class libraries) and intellectual. An early example of this approach was made by J. D. Carsley[102] who insisted as early as 1953 that there should be forty to fifty *enjoyable* books in every English classroom. Similarly David Holbrook's books contained reading lists which attempted to move away from a concentration on nineteenth-century novels of adventure. Some kind of seal was put on this search when Frank Whitehead, as Chairman of N.A.T.E. coined the phrase 'Literature broadly conceived' in addressing the 1966 Conference on 'Literature and Eng. Lit.'. Here an explicit contrast with the out-of-touch class reader was pointed up with the important criterion in selection being that the book should offer 'a mode of experience that has a very real bearing on our living, on our capacity for living; on the quality of our living'.[103] The invitation of the title is to extend literature outside a small handful of texts, maturely satisfying, for close textual reading; instead of 'knowledge about', what was sought was literature which 'enlarges the boundaries of awareness'

76

and 'influences the continually shifting balance of impulses and drives which are at war within us'.

In searching out books with these characteristics an obvious difficulty presents itself. Since the criteria relate to inner psychic change, how do we know that a particular book is influencing awareness in the right kind of way (we seek sympathy for the *right* thing, which raises the question of the nature of 'right')? What these new ideas did, in fact, was to raise questions of quality as the canon was extended. Nor was it possible simply to accept the judgement of time, accepted views about particular books, since the criteria had never before been applied to the whole corpus of writing. Even such judgements of 'greatness' conceded by academics have to be reconsidered in every generation. A great deal of hard work was promised, if the increase in variety was not to result in an incoherent jumble. However the hard work was to be welcomed because of the strong attachment to the experience of, and response to, literature as a staple ingredient of English lessons.

Criteria and Debate

Some criteria in making the extended choice of suitable books were offered by Michael Tucker in the same edition of N.A.T.E. Bulletin. 'Children should only be given good books, works of honesty, maturity; not books that pander or distort. . . . Our job as teachers is one of discrimination. What children read should be art not entertainment.'[104]

The to-and-fro of argument was very lively in the following years as new candidates for inclusion were proposed or rejected. Was for instance John Rowe Townsend speaking to our children with honesty, or was he condescending?

Interestingly enough, John Dixon gave no consideration to this question in *Growth through English*. His major stress was to suggest that literature be understood to include children's writing but he did not look to a widening list of books or offer any criteria. Perhaps his book was too theoretical for us to expect this. Perhaps, too, Dixon's (and Dartmouth's) attempt to hive off the literary critical/Eng. Lit. approach took up the major attention. Nevertheless John Dixon was offering a view of education which stressed the learner and learning, so the question of criteria in selecting books for children was very germane. It is an omission characteristic of his book. On the other hand, the particular 'child-centred' quality of his book would seem to imply support for a widening search for material felt to be relevant, quite outside the limits of books, as Leslie Stratta called it 'a variety of methods and media'.

John Dixon did return to a consideration of literature in English teaching. In a book published in 1973 *Patterns of Language*,[105] Dixon, together with Leslie Stratta and Andrew Wilkinson, sought to explore a range of possibilities within English, drawing on their experience of workshops with teachers in Africa and Canada. The book makes interesting reading alongside *Growth through English*. Obviously the viewpoint presented was that of all three authors, not Dixon alone; even so Chapter 2 was rather more supportive for the place of literature than *Growth through English*, though it still retained a certain coolness, a lack of enthusiasm.

> For many teachers of English 'literature' is of central concern. For them the term suggests an approach to reading which is something more than merely passing the time, something more than losing oneself uncritically in worlds of imagination and fantasy, something more than the unalloyed experience of pleasure so characteristic of the younger pupil's fascination in books. It suggests, among other things, the developing of critical awareness, reflecting on what has been read, arranging abstractions about literature into an ordered framework.

Lest it might have seemed that the *authors* did not share this viewpoint (of many teachers), they went on '. . . we acknowledge the fact that most pupils are dependent on their teachers for their introduction to a wider range of enjoyment, awareness and understanding, and that teachers of English are right to argue from their own experience that a more sophisticated reading of literature can provide this wider enjoyment, can create new awareness, and can deepen understanding'.

This whole remark seems to assume the value of reading and to echo strongly the concern for evaluation that, for instance, Frank Whitehead had shown in *The Disappearing Dais*, though *Patterns of Language* like *Growth through English* did not discuss any criteria for that evaluation, only the methods of approach in English lessons. The book shared something else with Frank Whitehead, a concern for the pupil's own felt response to a novel, poem or play. There were a number of problems in trying to deepen a pupil's awareness, such as 'how to talk about literature in the classroom without losing touch with felt responses. . . . And there is the further problem of how to help pupils to respond personally, with increasing subtlety and complexity, and not merely bow to the mature, adult perceptions of their teachers or literary critics.'

This seems a very incisive recognition of the problem, an attempt to balance all aspects of effective reading and valuable learning; further, the three authors pointed out 'a teacher cannot merely hand over the responsibility for learning entirely to his pupils. To do this would be to abdicate from his responsibility to them.'

It was this same abdication that I have seen in many a classroom and have felt in many an English teacher at meetings of English teachers. It was an abdication made easier by the lack of an effective account of the role of the culture, the teacher and values. And though *Patterns of Language* looks at ways of developing deeper awareness, it does not sustain the authentic role of the teacher in all respects, particularly in how to *select* the books, *where* to lead the forming judgment. That said, *Patterns of Language* provided a stimulating collection of ways of dealing with literature in the classroom, mainly by means of requiring pupils to *present* in some sort of performance, some insights into what they were reading, such as a dramatic reading, a documentary or a radio version.

It is a commonplace to speak of this as a 'golden age of children's literature'; never before, it would seem, have so many writers turned to children as their audience. A good deal of the writing has been of high quality and in looking for wider reading such writers as Ian Serraillier, Phillipa Pearce, Frederick Grice, Joan Aiken were drawn into consideration. For example Brian Hankins, in 1968, quoted all the above, in an article concerned with the first three years of a secondary school, and said: 'All these books have in common the *sine qua non* of a vigorously told story, plus the compassion, perception and organizing ability of the writer who is an artist. . . .'[106]

The inclusion of 'a vigorously told story' shows, in mild form, a concern for the child as reader which, with the growth of the reluctant reader, became a dominating concern. However, Hankins' concern for quality is the equal of that of Michael Tucker.

The 'dangers' of including books of poor, even damaging quality had been cogently argued by Tucker in that same year. Stressing that 'If literature matters at all it is because it is one of the means by which children can grow up, extend their sympathies, deepen their insights into their own and other's conduct, share their anxieties and guilt with the world at large'[107] he criticized particularly *The Ship* by C. S. Forester, *Cider with Rosie* (Laurie Lee), *Rogue Male* (G. Household) and *The Go-between* (L. P. Hartley), all books in use in schools, on the grounds that they encourage an escape from the world rather than 'an arming for life'. Here again Michael Tucker highlighted an issue which can be seen to thread its way through discussions over the years.

Another approach was to stress the *enjoyment* of books by children as an essential aim. But, if enjoyment were necessary, was it all that mattered? If the enjoyment were self-indulgent, escapist, did it matter, so long as reading took place? Wouldn't such reading lead naturally on to better things? If the child, as David Holbrook believed, is the best judge of his 'psychic' needs, does not the teacher leave the choice to the child, to move where he will?

All this argues for a particular view of the child; either the child is seen as a very effective self-regulating organism in whom we may have complete faith; or the child is immature, may choose advisedly at times, learn from mistakes, but might too often be distracted into choices that are self-debilitating. A concentration on the optimistic view would argue for withdrawal of the teacher's intrusive and unnecessary guidance; pessimism would encourage a lack of patience with the mistakes of the child, a lack of restrained professional sympathy with the emerging perceptions and discrimination of the child. The bias of late has been towards a vague optimism, a hope that things would come right if only children were enjoying the books, a hope that is bound to be met with disappointment.

A query as to the limits of enjoyment as a criterion was raised by J. M. Batten in response to Brian Hankins. He pointed out that many pupils can 'show evidence of enjoyment' without showing 'any real understanding of why the child feels it'.[108] So, although enjoyment was an essential foundation, efforts must be made to extend the pupil into deepening awareness. Enjoyment alone would not do it; any such hopes would be disappointed. The teacher, according to Batten, could not absolve himself from responsibility to choose and influence.

The whole dilemma was summed up by Oliver Gaggs: 'the books which children choose to read and enjoy are usually not the books which teachers feel it would be good for them to read'.[109]

His answer to the problem veered towards a defended optimism, since there was, he claimed, no evidence that any 'bad' book does any actual harm. On the contrary, he stated that such reading played a substantial part in making him a reader and his own daughter was quoted to show that children do not absorb the moral value of the books they read (eg Buchan's racism).

Now the limited value of extrapolating from those 'hooked on books' to the general school population should be obvious. Nor, surely, is the danger with poor books that they transmit execrable moral values (that is to confuse literature with propaganda, and there are differences). Literature is concerned with *concrete* personal experience in its ebb and flow, inviting us to invest our sympathies or our resistance in particular acts. These may build up in a particular reader to a general guiding philosophy, but that is the act of the reader well divorced from the writer. The real danger is that the writer may not claim our honesty, integrity or justice, suborning our human dignity. What results is a general distortion of the flow of sympathy.

Nevertheless, in spite of these caveats, the importance of children's enjoyment and the value of reading in quantity, which Gaggs made a guiding rule, can be accepted. However, two illustrative examples of where enjoyment as the overriding aim may lead are to be found in articles by R. Sampson and Jane Powell in *English in Education*. Sampson presented the claims of science fiction for inclusion as a body. Indeed, 'only snobbery and ignorance . . . have prevented S.F. from being regarded with respect'.[110] However the qualities which are to gain the respect are not detailed; for the classroom, though, 'S.F. has three main advantages; it is cheap, popular and luridly packaged'. The approach to teaching which provides a context for this was made clear when Sampson listed the reasons for reading – pleasure, a trigger for ideas, to initiate writing, to stimulate an appetite for more, to improve mechanical skills and to encourage critical and irreverent thinking. Among all this 'S.F. is ideal; there is an endless supply, it is easy to read, cheap to buy and most S.F. novels are less than 200 pages'. The approach is very much that of consumer-satisfaction at its lowest level; if it goes down well, give it to them in large quantities.

Jane Powell looked particularly to contemporary fiction and especially to children's literature. She indicated that there was a lack of interest among pupils for reading, which would be accepted by most teachers of English and shown up in the Schools Council Project *Children's Reading Interests*. The greatest problem came with the truculence of the fourth form. However: 'The girls will read, most of them quite a lot, if the right books are available; first date, boyfriends, unmarried mums, drugs are nearly aways winners.' As for the boys 'Thrillers, horror stories, some S.F. and something like *Here we go Round the Mulberry Bush* . . . are the best bet. It's sex they go for, of course.'[111]

It is illuminating to contrast that way of cataloguing books (wholly 'subject', nothing of quality considered, popularity above all) with that of Michael Tucker. The difference is enormous, partly explained no doubt by the increasing need to compete directly with the commercial alternatives to education. The need for the involvement and interest of the child had become, by 1975, ingrained at a time when gaining the interest was more difficult than ever. At the same time the changes are directly a result of the search for a wider choice of reading matter, shorn of questions of quality. One wonders what is the point of reading 'rubbish'? Where is it supposed to lead? Is enjoyment always to be regarded as a valued end? I do not know of any evidence that reading *anything* leads to selection of quality, though a voracious reader who reads good and bad does have the basis for mature discrimination. It seems to me an over-hopeful approach, justified perhaps as a survival measure in difficult circumstances, but certainly not to be offered as the way forward. I do not feel we need be so desperate.

Research and Reading

The Dartmouth Conference had projected the need for research into the teaching of literature 'and a longitudinal study of children's response to literature'.[112] Since then there have been three research projects into different aspects of literature.

In 1967 there began a 'Project concerned with Literature (Prose Books) in English Teaching between the ages of eleven and sixteen'. Eventually giving rise to a report *Reading Together* on the use of readers, the project was researched by Kenyon Calthop (who wrote the report) and directed by Frank Whitehead. The general intention was to diffuse information of good practice; the background assumption was that 'Informed opinion at the present time is agreed about the centrality of literature (broadly conceived) in the teaching of English, and stress has rightly been laid, in many quarters, on the importance for children's personal and linguistic development of the experience they obtain from reading.'[113] The book proved to be a useful resource book for teachers.

The *Children as Readers* Project, directed initially by Douglas Barnes for the Schools Council and N.A.T.E. had the intention of studying 'the roles of literature in the curriculum of the Primary and Secondary School'. The intention in 1968 was to make the working of the project rather loose, and unfortunately the resultant findings some six years later were too diffuse and shapeless for the Schools Council to publish. Looking back, this seems a great pity since the project absorbed the efforts of a lot of committed teachers, of whom I was one, who saw nothing at the end but the water running into the sand. The result was a weakened sense of purpose and no signs of a public voice. The hopes and excitement which we had at the start of our working party on 'Poetry in the middle years', which occupied us for many months, needed a place in some coherent overall framework. All contacts with the co-ordinating figures seemed to reinforce our own sense of isolation, rather than belonging. An action/research project *can* create cohesion and solidarity among participating teachers so that they are lifted into further thought and effort. (An example here is the series of projects on *writing* carried out by the London University Institute of Education team, based on the Britton schema of language uses.) Perhaps a successful outcome to the *Children as Readers* Project would have had a marked effect on the direction of change. As it was Douglas Barnes found a stronger interest in the language of the classroom and resigned long before the Project had run its course, a move which exemplified the time's exciting new areas of interest.

The third project concentrated on the children, their likes and dislikes, and especially their changing patterns of reading as they proceed through adolescence. Directed, again, by Frank Whitehead during its life (1969–74), the Project, *Children's Reading Interests*, came to the depressing conclusion that reading as a habit or interest declines strongly through the years of compulsory schooling; however, there was some sign that the right kind of stimulation, knowledge and interest from the teacher could have an impact on that trend. Throughout, Frank Whitehead's assurance of the value of reading 'quality' literature was strong.

In the full report *Children and their Books*[114] there emerged a picture indicating that many English teachers did not see the children's reading of full books as their province. There was a sizeable proportion of teachers using theme work, and extracts, though this, as might be expected, did not encourage the children to read books. It was as if the organizational requirements of teaching excluded one of the major purposes of the whole enterprise. As the report commented: '. . . if the development of wide independent reading is a central or important goal of English teaching (and surely this should be axiomatic), then this objective is most effectively attained by a concentration in English lessons upon the reading of "real" books (novels, stories and other complete prose books) rather than by the study of extracts.'

It is worth asking how teachers could have come to the position where the 'axiomatic' goal could be so clearly forgotten.

The report saw the reading of books as an exercise in choice and opportunity: 'children greatly value the opportunity given to them by book reading to exercise their own choice and to pursue highly individual interests and tastes through books' and then went on to suggest that 'The great and continuing strength of the book in its competition with the audio-visual media is, in fact, its unrivalled ability to give the individual the chance to follow his own particular bent at any one particular time, to engage actively rather than passively with the medium. . . . The opportunity for self-discovery and self-realization opened up by books seems to us an integral and central component in any conception of education which takes personal growth as its goal.'

This makes an interesting contrast with those teachers who have seen reading as more constricting than writing or have seen reading and literature as a largely indoctrinatory pursuit. If reading confers *increased* freedom it should surely be a goal central to all schools and all teachers. Yet the project found a depressing proportion of schools which 'expressed only minimal pretensions to a concern about their pupils' voluntary reading'.

The report stressed throughout the real difference made to a child's reading development by knowledgeable, sensitive encouragement from teachers; where this was absent, the amount of reading was less. The encouragement, in turn, for the teacher, is there. We do have an effect if we take this goal seriously; conversely we cannot shift the responsibility onto others (the ethos of the school, the environment, etc).

At the heart of the report was a chapter called 'The books children prefer' which sought among other things to account for what reading brings to a child reader – what the child seeks and what the child gains. There was a study of the contribution of D. W. Harding to understanding the process of reading; this is, incidentally, a critique of James Britton's use of Harding, for it points out his (Harding's) inclusion of *evaluation* in the role of the onlooker: 'Part of everyone's time is spent in looking on at events, not primarily in order to understand them, but in a non-participant relation *which yet includes an active evaluative attitude.*' (Harding, quoted p. 218. My italics.)

However the project team felt that reading is more complex and involves two main elements – imaginative sharing (identification and wish-fulfilment) and evaluative judgment – that is, it is larger than Harding's 'role of the onlooker'. The precise relationship between the two elements remains to be explored.

As for the impact of the projects as a whole it would probably be true to say that it has not been great. It may be that the area of study was not novel, no frontiers were being crossed and the mood of the sixties and early seventies seems, looking back, to have been innovative to a fault. Perhaps the work will be recognised at its worth at a later time. Certainly there seems now to be a burgeoning wish to reconsider the conclusions of the last fifteen years. These projects into literature teaching are by no means reactionary; indeed they suggest quite radical changes. Their *assumptions* are however largely the same as, say, Denys Thompson in the early sixties.

Fight the good fight
The supportive background for this continuing look at literature was in the writings of Denys Thompson, the *Use of English* journal and the advocacy of Frank Whitehead, who, as we have already seen, played a central role in the research projects. Frank Whitehead has maintained throughout 'the experience of literature has a role to play which is absolutely central and integral to this growth-process'.[115] His repeated appearance throughout these pages testifies sufficiently to his deep

involvement, though other voices have increasingly been found by many more relevant to the times. The basis of his advocacy is quite simply that literature is so important, so valuable, that it must have the most important place in English, *whether or not* some unified theory can be found to justify it in relation to the rest. He has come nearest to such a justifying account and this can be set over against that of James Britton (and after him John Dixon). Britton's is a neater theory, more intellectually satisfying in its inclusiveness; Whitehead's is more complete and less tidy. Both are in the end unsatisfactory.

Another whose writing gave support to the place of literature was Sidney Bolt, who united the *sine qua non* of personal response with a strong belief in the value of what literature has to offer. His book[116] was contemporary with Whitehead's *The Disappearing Dais* and has been referred to already. It is sufficient here to repeat that Bolt, working in Further Education, began with reading for the 'fictitious experience' as a basis for discussion and writing, progressing to a more concentrated 'experience of reading'. Though he was at pains (typical of those times) to separate his approach from 'teaching English Literature' he did apparently support attention to the page, to the unique quality of the created work. Bolt did not construct a coherent theory, only argued a personal style of teaching. When he came to write in 1967 he maintained the distinction between literature as social study (source of experience to talk about) and literature as literature, asserting 'They (students) cannot be left to make their own mistakes' about that.[117] He was sensitive to the quality of some literature, which refuses to succumb to the notion of English as 'experience' but demands its own terms.

Bolt developed these points further (there is a noticeable development in his writing) in a joint work with Roger Gard.[118] Here he complained of those 'teachers and theorists' who 'bring literature out of its own sufficiencies and into a close and improper embrace with what they call 'experience'. This is the start of an extended critique of *Growth through English* with its 'comprehensive cluster of activities': '. . . the critical reading of imaginative literature is one of them and must not be blended with the others. . . . It should be the chief means and the great end of English study at any level. And it seems strange that in a climate which values "awareness" so much, the most potently aware of human activities, literature, should be compounded with a mess of unorganized experience.'

The major criticism of Dixon was, as might be expected, aimed at the linguistic notion of literature as language 'in the role of spectator'. '*Growth through English* is based on the theory that since language is the principal means whereby humanity structures Reality, English teaching is concerned with the apprehension of Reality in all its forms. And its naïve objection to fiction as fiction is that it is not Reality.... Literature was defined as a means of apprehending Reality.... The basic error is the failure to recognize the fact that the word "literature" implies a valuation.' And finally 'Mr. Dixon's thought is governed by a series of stringent either/ors. As he sees it the only alternative to his method is "looking at life through fictions" and taking no interest in Reality'.

Bolt saw, it appears, a deep hostility to literature in its own right in both Dixon and the theory he presented, based unequivocally on James Britton's 'virtual experience' without any accompanying evaluation. This comment makes for an illuminating comparison with Frank Whitehead, echoing his concern for literature and for its evaluations, yet rejecting the notion of 'experience' to which Whitehead seems to subscribe. They both concur in their respect for the achievement of quality in literature; in the surety, that is, that there are important criteria by which literature is judged beyond anything merely personal.

At the beginning of *Teaching Fiction in Schools*, Bolt and Gard acknowledged their debt to F. R. Leavis, an allegiance to whose ideas unites several of those who, after Dartmouth, tried to recreate the case for literature. (Ironically the American party at Dartmouth saw the English there as mainly disciples of Leavis.) This was certainly true of Fred Inglis who weighed in in swashbuckling style on several occasions. We have already seen him in action against *Language in Use*. In his approach to literature Inglis saw it as 'the redemptive experience of the private soul', ambitious in the quest for mature civilized life. His experience in higher education has probably influenced his level of expectation. At an earlier time he spoke of English as 'cultivating the growth of values. These values only live, are exchanged, deepened, and enriched by language.'[119] His 'research project' was intended to show up the kinds of values that children were taking away from school, particularly a sense of place, a sense of the past, a tenderness for people and a response to the quality of life in language. In all of these, Inglis claimed, literature played a paramount part. By the time he wrote up the report, *The Englishness of English Teaching*, he had added the values of a sense of coherence and powers of discrimination, and explicitly stressed the 'literary-critical' interpretative skills in English teaching. He, like Frank Whitehead, found strong evidence that the teachers had an immense power; those who sought high achievement saw it realized. The high achievement was by way of quality literature. Surprisingly seeing the textbook *Reflections* as a direct descendant of *Culture and Environment* by Leavis and Denys Thompson, he nevertheless shares with others I have mentioned a sense of the cultural heritage which exists in the form of literature; he contrasts this with the society around him in a style reminiscent of Denys Thompson. 'Our present society traduces and insults much of the humanity we live by and are. It enforces still and obdurate relations; it drains and distorts aspiration; it prevents an upright and spontaneous dignity. . . . Unconsciously rather than as a policy of planned robbery, the mass of the people of England have been disinherited of their living cultural heritage.'[120]

Fred Inglis speaks out of the tradition, critical of industrial society, of Leavis and Thompson and like them he insists on the place of literature in countering that culture and discovering personal worth. From this stance the influence of a socio-linguistic theory which omits value seems intellectual betrayal. Hence his criticisms of Doughty and Britton.

Another writer, admirer of Leavis, to battle against the 'new' concentration on language was Arthur Capey, who took part in a long battle on the issue in the columns of the *Use of English* with J. R. Osgerby about the English course in a teacher-training college. Osgerby described a course heavily arranged in Themes-and-Activities and looking in an apologetic way outside the literary-critical.[121] A good deal of doubt was expressed about the traditional course, with its concentration on close study and appreciation of the classics. Arthur Capey criticized the outlined course in many respects but the main point was that 'the central purpose of Main English is to extend and deepen the student's capacity vicariously to know, to feel, to experience and personally to judge and discriminate'.[122] In this purpose, the study of literature is vital. 'If students are to become personally sensitive to language and increasingly competent in their use of it, . . . how else then through the study of literature and the cultivation of the literary-critical habit are they to become so?'

At this juncture Capey makes a criticism which penetrates deeply into the language-based approach to English: '. . . there is a kind of neutrality in evidence today which pretends to "objectivity" the further implication being that "objectivity" represents truth or at least the search for it while "subjectivity" stemming from the person, represents upbringing, schooling, "class assumptions", prejudice and hence untruth or at least an unwillingness to seek the truth'.

A course which relegates literature to a subsidiary role is rejecting the key aim of *evaluation*, as far as Capey is concerned. With values included, no present theory of language can account for them, not even such a comprehensive one as Britton's.

In total, the writings of Whitehead, Bolt, Inglis and Capey show a

reluctance to be convinced of the adequacy of the Dixon/Britton
language theory, especially regarding literature. They were not alone in
that but have been selected as authoritative examples. However the
general tone of their remarks has been increasingly defensive against
the onward march of the Dixon/Britton theory, sometimes even strident,
as if the audience has moved away.

Chapter 8

Coming home to roost

Since 1966 there have been occasional criticisms of the *Growth through English* position, many of which have been mentioned already. What has been lacking has been a thoroughgoing discussion of these criticisms or any shift in the dominating theory to take account of these criticisms. As far back as 1973, J. A. M. Baldwin in an article called 'Growth through English'[123] made many of the important criticisms in a defence of the possibilities of literature, properly approached. Perhaps he forecast all too accurately the response he was to receive, for there was no response: 'the disciples of the new orthodoxy will view attempts to maintain its [literature's] centrality in the classroom as the desperate efforts at a rearguard action by middle-class philanthropists distributing baskets of apples to the deserving poor'.

He suggested that he was presenting a *positive* critique by concluding: 'It is a pity that in a book which presents so many convincing points and which must be causing so many practising teachers to think again about the whole rationale of their work in English, Mr Dixon should neglect the potentiality of literature as a point of growth in the classroom and as one means whereby the pupil can experience the possibilities of language in operation.'

Baldwin was perhaps not regarded by those who were developing the 'growth' model as sufficiently known to demand response (but then, neither were Capey, Bolt, or Inglis). Albert Kitzhaber was a participant at Dartmouth; his 'A rage for disorder'[124] had a tinge of nostalgia, a wish to return to a pre-Dartmouth position, which is neither possible nor desirable. Perhaps it was that unrealistic wish which prevented his criticisms being taken up.

The point I wish to stress is that the criticisms that have been made from time to time of the thinking that has come so much to dominate English teaching since Dartmouth have not usually been felt to require response. There has been very little discussion or debate – rather it has seemed like an excited orthodoxy too busy developing its own approaches to react to the sniping from the flanks. It is important to realize that there have been repeated opportunities for debate when we come to consider more recent attempts to criticise the positions of John Dixon and James Britton. If there is no response to a criticism, the critic is likely to become more strident, seeking *some* reaction; or the critic may rebound to associate with others who share the same criticisms. Either way chances have been lost for creative disagreement.

It was, I suggest, no great surprise that the unresolved issues of 1966 should be taken up again sooner or later. The most thoroughgoing attempt to date to reopen the discussions of Dartmouth was made by Frank Whitehead in 1976 and 1978, when in *Use of English* he published two articles, polemical in tone, concerned with the Dixon/Britton model of English. The first one, 'Stunting the growth'[125] was concerned with the contribution of John Dixon, especially in *Growth through English*. The second 'What's the use, indeed?'[126], with James Britton and his language model.

Whitehead related the developments of the sixties to the change in morale of the seventies. In the sixties, 'The English teachers I knew and respected . . . believed . . . that English teaching was a unity, but that the experience of literature, broadly conceived, must be an absolutely central component of that unity – almost, one might say, the corner-stone upon which the arch depended.' I have earlier commented on this use of 'central' and the nature of 'literature, broadly conceived'. I have also shown how Whitehead has been throughout a spokesman for these same teachers.

However, he described a change in English teaching so profound that 'the beginning English teacher today moves into a scene which is riven by factions, uncertain, confused, lacking a clear sense of direction, often dispirited, sometimes betraying signs of a malaise which comes perilously close to demoralization'.

It certainly seems harder to teach English today; many agree on that. Pat D'Arcy, a member of the University of London Institute of Education Writing Project Team, found a number of changes when she returned to the classroom. 'What is forgotten (or repressed?) once out of the classroom is above all the element of confrontation. . . . Of all the stresses that teachers have to contend with nowadays, I would put at the top this direct challenge to their right to demand the commitment of the whole class to the activities they have to offer.'[127]

This confrontation makes any kind of teaching difficult; it is doubly difficult to work in those areas which require patience, suspension of judgement, an imaginative leap, which are the kinds of demands that any serious teaching of English must involve.

Whitehead catalogued the problems from outside English that have made teaching more difficult but added that the book *Growth through English* had 'helped to compound our present difficulties'. He revealed a profound disappointment in the Dartmouth Seminar ('. . . there was very little meeting of minds'). He had been centrally involved in the assembly of the British contingent and in the acceptance of the invitation; obviously his disappointment was made all the stronger by his own sense of direct responsibility.

He described the seminar in progress. 'In such a bemused intellectual climate, what tends to happen is that simplistic notions at a high level of abstraction are seized upon with relief as common ground – common ground the implications of which can, of course, be interpreted very differently according to the prepossessions of the different parties.' His view of the seminar was, then, more akin to that of Denys Thompson and James Miller than John Dixon or James Britton. As examples of the abstract simplistic notions, Whitehead mentioned Dixon's three 'models' of English teaching and James Britton's division of language into 'spectator role' or 'participant role' (the subject of 'What's the use, indeed?').

However, as 'the most disastrous' idea, Whitehead nominated 'the wide definition of literature . . . which assimilated "pupils' stories and poems" ("the literature of the classroom") to the mature products of real authors'. He carefully conceded that children's writing is or can be, 'continuous' with that of mature writers but that the Dartmouth definition went beyond that, 'to insinuate, in effect, a higher educational value for children's talk and writing than for their reading of "real" literature'. About the *influence* of this definition of literature, Whitehead was quite clear. He saw a direct effect on English teaching for '. . . since Dartmouth, the wider definition has lent sanction to an effective denigration of the experience of literature. . . . Increasingly literature has been "used".' That is, 'used' in the service of some other element, such as talk, writing or social relevance, or 'used' merely as a trigger to set off exchange of first-hand experience.

'All these now-fashionable activities seem to me to imply an erosion of belief in the power of literature as such, in the value of exposing oneself to the impact of a poem, or story or novel for its own sake.' Perhaps here he had in mind the kinds of activities suggested in *Patterns of Language*, which, while they are useful additions to the teacher's armoury, do tend to assume that a straightforward encounter with a work of literature, a reading, is insufficient.

There seems to me to be a good deal of accuracy in Whitehead's description of 'an erosion of belief'. One result has been that teachers have given too little thought to reading and literature, in particular to the problem of how to encourage a personal response which is also an informed response. Many, perhaps most, have settled for either any reaction as valid, or a predigested response passed from teacher to pupil. (There is a lot of such teaching, especially in preparation for the 'rigour' of public literature examinations.)

Enthusiasts have become strident; doubters have become opponents. I feel also that good literature teaching has probably been made even more difficult because it has often felt it necessary to take up an inflexible, intransigent position. (Not that good literature teaching has disappeared; it has, though, had to rely on strong character rather than widespread informing discussion.)

Whitehead felt that these difficulties were, if not caused by Dixon and Dartmouth, certainly exacerbated by them, because of the failure to give an adequate role for literature in the 'growth' model. Furthermore he criticized Dixon for another defeat in the book: '. . . although there is extensive mention of the micro-society of the classroom, there is nowhere any real analysis of the macro-society within which classroom and school have their being'. As a result, the book has nothing to say about the reductive influences to which children are subject, especially from the entertainments industry, to which English teachers must define their attitude.

I have tried to develop the contention that English teaching is inevitably concerned with values and with the culture outside the classroom. I have criticized *Growth through English* myself for its failure to grapple with these two dimensions. However, even accepting the need to define an attitude to the 'media', there remain such problems as *how* to relate to the fact that children's view of reality is so strongly moulded by hours of television. What are we to do in response to the deep involvement of the majority of children in pop-star cults?

These are matters that impinge directly on the child's growth to adulthood and are concerned all the time with evaluation and perspective. They directly influence the ability of the child to explore the unfamiliar, to sustain interest over a long period, to savour quiet pleasures. Pop cults involve admiration for a rootless, aimless sort of life, of cynicism and self-destruction.

English teachers need to define an attitude which cannot be indifferent or compliant. The 'growth' model does not relate English work to these issues and so does not help towards that definition. By its omission it has allowed English teachers to believe indifference or compliance are possible. Indeed it seems now that pop-music is the music of many teachers; universities are on the circuit for pop-groups; the words of pop-songs are regarded by many as literature.

In the second of his two articles, Frank Whitehead turned to the language categories of James Britton. He acknowledged 'the positive merits of Britton's work' but had come 'to believe that in the real world of English teaching Britton's influence has been disturbingly harmful'.

A good proportion of Whitehead's criticism was based on the way Britton had used his sources, in such a way, according to Whitehead, as to show that Britton was simplifying the ideas taken on and even language itself. The major criticisms were:

—That Britton's theories are over-ambitious in dividing all language into that in the role of participant and that in the role of spectator.

—That '"valuing" and "judging" is an activity which he shies away from'.

—That the idea of the continuity of 'gossip' and 'literature' 'exalts the significance in human life of the former and at the same time subtly denigrates the distinctive characteristics of the latter'.

—That the idea of 'poetic' advanced by Britton stresses *form*, which is not the way literature works. ('Isn't the only "form" which counts for anything in "art-speech" that which is significant because it is an embodiment of *values*?')

—That 'Britton's brand of theorizing has created a climate which encourages teachers to believe that when they have assigned their pupils' language to a category, or covered all the modes, they have accomplished something.[128] I would contend that what is far more important is to evaluate responsibly, to be able to spot what is good (whatever its kind or category) and to reward and reinforce the growing-point with unstinted praise.'

I began by suggesting that the teaching of the seventies has been influenced by the ideas and publications of the sixties. In studying the discussions at the Dartmouth Seminar I showed how the report by John Dixon failed to draw in all the voices that were there. Even more the model that was offered *could not* account for a number of essential elements.

Frank Whitehead's articles were a belated attempt to rectify those omissions and to reject some of the recent developments in the light of their effects (He seems to find little valuable in what is distinctively Britton.) Retrospectively, those effects now seem predictable, yet I know from my own experience that the implications took time to emerge clearly.

Whitehead's comments were retrospective, seeing past events influential on later ones. They were, moreover, quite new in tone and point of attack (John Dixon was certainly surprised by them), though there had been, as I have shown, some critical rumblings from others. In total, his critique was more thoroughgoing than had ever been made at Dartmouth or elsewhere in the public sphere. Yet they were attempting to take up issues which had been in evidence already in the sixties, and which I have tried to relate to an unsuccessful attempt to create an adequate unified theory of English. It is literature which has been the main casualty in practice, as Frank Whitehead clearly believed.

It would be easy to say that Frank Whitehead should have been making these remarks in the sixties, not in 1976 and 1978 (some have said so, and I certainly wish he had). However it is only recently that the implications of the theory have been clear. A number of people have had partial insight but no-one has been able to relate cause and effect so firmly. Another problem has been the lack of a forum. There has been an energetic orthodoxy at work developing the Dixon/Britton model (it has been very powerful in generating new thought) so busily that qualification or criticism has been impatiently received or ignored. My own experience has been puzzling here. Time and again major figures involved in the development of work following out the ramifications of the Dixon/Britton model of language have confessed privately to me doubts and reservations, which publicly, in lecture, book or seminar, they do not admit, as if there is no room for them in the scope of the ongoing work. I have heard almost all Frank Whitehead's criticisms voiced by such figures, but privately.

Thus I have heard criticized: the inadequacy of the *poetic* category; the omission of questions of quality; the exaggerated claims for talk; the fragmentary nature of much English teaching under the influence of the Dixon/Britton model; the orthodoxy of such a body as N.A.T.E; the lack of discussion on the casualties of the new thinking.

Let me be clear. This is not an accusation of either cowardice or conspiracy. I believe this reticence to be a direct result of two parallel forces. The theory not only failed to include all the important elements but it also made it very difficult to reconsider their place *without destroying the whole theory* (it is often the nature of a theory that it either holds or it crumbles).

The second influence has been the loyalty between the small number of people at the thinking forefront of the 'growth' theory. There is a real freemasonry, based on genuine respect and liking. This is, obviously, preferable to an aggressive competitiveness, yet it has the drawback of forbidding rethinking that involves criticism of one's professional friends.

Clearly John Dixon felt Frank Whitehead had belonged to that loyal freemasonry and was considerably hurt by the article criticizing his contribution. He was perhaps even more hurt by the criticisms of James Britton, by whom he has been deeply influenced and whom he counts as a close friend.

There is a story that when Whitehead's first article was published the executive of N.A.T.E. considered responding *as an association*, defending John Dixon. In the event, of course, John Dixon was more than capable of responding for himself, but the feeling in N.A.T.E was that it was a *personal* attack on an eminent figure.

Defence under attack
There had been no response to Baldwin, Bolt or Inglis. John Dixon responded to Frank Whitehead, rather belatedly.[129] Characteristically he had not rushed to reply to the criticisms of himself; his reply does not concern itself with the first article at all. He took up the criticisms of James Britton, though he confessed to there being 'two articles by Frank Whitehead in recent issues that I very much regret'. The source of his regret was that the articles had purported to be critical analyses of recent theoretical work but that in them 'critical care had been abandoned' because the *tone* of the articles was 'the language of advocacy and persuasion; it leaves little room for the reader to make up his own mind. . . .'

His second response was to regret the way the matter was polarized into *sides*. There was certainly evidence in the articles for this polarization; Dixon was able to demonstrate this clearly. He implied however that there are no sides in the discussion, that this was a regrettable contribution from Frank Whitehead himself. Yet the very criticisms that were made by Whitehead had been lurking, taking shape since the sixties, indeed *generated* inevitably by the incomplete theory. There *has* been an orthodoxy too excited by its own activities to think back to the beginning. A comparison of the *Use of English* with *English in Education* in the seventies will reveal a divergence largely into those who are comfortable with the Dixon/Britton model and those who are not. N.A.T.E. conferences tend to sustain that orthodoxy, though there are strong criticisms voiced. The failure of N.A.T.E. to increase its numbers dramatically is to an extent due, I feel, to the belief of outsiders that it is not for all teachers of English, but only for those who accept the orthodoxy. However that caricatures the true position, it does have some connection with the reality. The fact is worth noting that two years after the publication of 'Stunting the Growth', there has been no discussion in *English in Education* of the issues that were raised, as if either they do not matter or the polemical nature of the article were off-putting. It is a silence that suggests 'sides'.

John Dixon completed his reply by attempting to reinstate Britton's use of his sources (only a careful reading of these sources and Britton's use of them can answer here) and then invited further discussion:

'. . . there is not enough critical exchange at present about recent attempts to offer a theoretical foundation for work in English – or in langage development'. However, John Dixon did not apparently see Frank Whitehead's articles as party to this critical exchange, for he did not respond to a number of the criticisms made.

A first step, surely, ought to be to examine the criticisms – whether or not their tone is regrettable. John Dixon did not, in his reply to Frank Whitehead, address himself to the criticisms of the language model itself, of the *denigration* of literature, of the confusion of gossip and literature, of the substitution of a checklist of categories for a concern for quality. Instead, he tried to defend James Britton's professional and personal integrity, an act of generosity but not advancing the critical exchange much farther.

The survey of the writing of English teaching over recent years compels the view that Frank Whitehead's two articles actually originated in the sixties, when, however, they could not have been written. They are some of the pigeons of the sixties coming home to roost. What had been necessary in the meanwhile was the testing out of the Dixon/ Britton approach to English for its strengths and its weaknesses. (Its strengths remain and must be retained in any reformulations.) There does not yet, unfortunately, seem to be mutual comprehension between the advocates and critics of the theory – which means that there must inevitably be 'sides'. If there remains no forum for discussion, the two 'sides' will drift apart, even perhaps go to different courses and conferences (the D.E.S. and N.A.T.E. Conferences seem already to be composed of very differing clientele). Silence cannot be mistaken for consent.

What must be firmly retained is the importance of the child's response, the child's learning, and the frequent discontinuity between what actually happens in the child and what the teacher thinks happens, for we need to know how to bring these together. James Britton and John Dixon have played a vital role in making us sensitive to the child's end of teaching and learning.

Chapter 9

English is not all language

English through the sixties and seventies has looked outwards and drawn into itself an increasing range of approach and content. The subject English has extended its boundaries into language, so that many English teachers see no need to distinguish between the kind of work that is done in English lessons and the language element in all learning. Indeed I have heard English teachers express a loss of interest in English as a subject and a preference to involve themselves with wider curricular matters – language across the curriculum or language in learning.

The range of approaches to English, the variety of items included, is very extensive and still increasing, in spite of the counter-pressures to reduce the subject to 'basics'. For instance there are those now who see the future of English in the form of 'communications', in which even language is seen as only one form of communication. Presumably in such a growth, there may be a new danger that *language* is treated as merely one among equals. This is a debate to be heard in the next few years in the field of English 16–19.

This urge to subsume elements under one head, an urge that has been very powerful of late and which I have called 'the drive to inclusiveness', is part of the total attempt to proclaim the unity of all learning. This drive to see similarities, connexions, has of course been valuable. The rigid separation of the curriculum into subjects in the secondary school has led to an inbuilt failure to work in the fruitful areas between subjects. In addition it has meant that the common element of language in all subjects has been allowed to remain acknowledged and thus untreated. The recent moves to break down the barriers between subjects and within subjects (eg English is concerned with all language) has led to a ferment of ideas, a revaluation of established practice, a discovery of many more suitable materials, more suitable that is to the pupils, the times and the kind of learning being sought. No good teacher can afford to ignore the wealth of ideas that have emerged, particularly under the conception of the 'unity' of English.

However this ferment and expansion has been going on long enough now for a revaluation of itself in its own turn, and two caveats need to be presented.

Firstly, the drive to see *similarities* between the elements of English, or indeed all elements of language, can lead to us ignoring *differences*, unique qualities in the separate elements, which are part of their very life. Thus, reading is different to writing, which is different to speaking. There are, we must see, important distinctions between the words of poetry and the language of 'urban studies', which are not merely a matter of style, or even of register. Nor is all poetry the same. An essential distinction is between poetry which is true to life and poetry which is self-regarding, essentially dishonest.

It seems in the process of making connexions, we might have lost from our attention these essential kinds of differences. So, in English, what are the *distinctive* elements upon which we ought to concentrate? Are there any indeed that we relinquish at our peril, educationally speaking?

The second warning concerns *relationships* between elements. The Bullock Report[130] based its deliberations on 'the principle that reading, writing, talking and listening should be treated as a unity'.

The principle can be seen as of the same ancestry of other such expressions in the sixties. For example, Peter Abbs wrote: 'literature, drama, discussion, research, writing, all run into each other, parts that form the whole'.[131] However, the unity of these elements cannot, without damage, be insisted upon without a corresponding recognition of their *distinctness*. And it is in the *relationship* of one element to another that the unity and distinctness are safeguarded. If reading is treated as the same as talk, only absurdity will result. If we approach reading and forget its distinctive qualities we shall fail to draw out its central potencies. There will, therefore, be times when the particular activity, be it talking, listening, reading or writing, will be seen to demand its own rightful treatment before we go off onto another, with its own complementary but different requirements and strengths.

It is in the careful recognition of the relationships between the different modes of language, that we shall find a coherent unity, such as was not established in the sixties, either by those who argued for literature or by those who sought a language nexus. Nobody since has succeeded in establishing that unity because no-one has satisfied the two criteria most noticeably absent – interrelationship and values. That is, how do the various aspects of English relate to the whole and what are they all for in the end?

For instance, if talk is an essential element in English, we need to establish what kinds of talk. What is the connexion of talk with writing and reading? What are the valuable kinds of talk and why? How does the talk in English lessons relate to the kind of talk we seek in the adult world? A good deal of encouragement of talk in English has assumed the value of talk for its own sake, children being allowed to choose any way of talking which they feel relevant and meaningful for them. Of course, this often leads to energetic, purposeful talk but just as often it leads into sterile, self-defeating wrangles or vaporous exchanges of peer-group clichés. What are we to make of the Head of English who gleefully relates how other departments in his school looked askance at him, because they believed talk should have a purpose, while he thought any talk at all was bound to be valuable, however apparently pointless or even destructive of some other enterprise, such as reading or writing? Such anarchic extremes are allowed by the general failure to relate talk to the other elements or to the overall purposes of English.

We teachers of English have to select what we attend to from the whole range of possibilities, and if our overall principles do not guide us in that selection on the basis of priorities, then we will select merely on personal preference, avoiding what we do not like so well, doing a great deal of work on our enthusiasms. This has been encouraged by the common belief that it is the teacher's enthusiasm which makes for good teachers; conversely no amount of coercion or dutiful compliance will produce meaningful teaching. I believe this to have some truth but such a faith in personal enthusiasm needs to be qualified. A teacher's enthusiasm can be *created* by understanding, by grasp of the overall intention; enthusiasm can be misplaced so that whim is thought to be sufficient.

There are, whether we like it or not, imperatives in teaching – there must be a purpose and we must select our approaches accordingly. Our enthusiasms must be up for scrutiny.

We must, too, scrutinize what really goes on in our lessons. The work here of Douglas Barnes and others has made us uncomfortable, sometimes to the extent of rendering teachers incapable of confident action. Such scrutiny is, nevertheless, an essential in teaching, whether it be by means of filming lessons, allowing other teachers to observe, or by some self-examination. (I suggest all of these – the last whether or not the others are tried.) Children can play the game of guessing what teacher wants from a question or from a mode of working. In small-group discussion, are the children actually discussing the poem or are they pretending to? The problem with a lot of the teacher-free work that we have taken into our new style is that we know even less on a day-to-day basis what the children are actually learning than we know of the teacher-dominated lessons, since we can observe so little of it, and the balance of gain and loss is so difficult to assess. For example what proportion of a discussion that wanders, includes personal animosity and frustration, returns to the subject fitfully and so on is convincingly valuable? I suggest we do not know the answers, cannot, unless we can relate that to other talk, later talk, attitudes to reading, stamina in writing and many more elements of our work. We have not related them because we have not felt the need to do so – enjoyment or personal interest has been all.

This failure to interrelate the elements of English was already there in the sixties, compounded by a failure to distinguish between English and language. These interrelationships were felt as problems before and during the Dartmouth Seminar; *Growth through English*, and subsequently *Language and Learning*, were thought to have satisfactorily solved those problems. But they did not and could not because they had no satisfactory explanation of the role of the past or the role of values in the culture in which the learning takes place.

Some of the images that have been used in writing and thinking on English have apparently contributed to the confusion and delayed clarity of thought or purpose. 'Centre', 'central', 'map', 'process', 'models', 'growth' – these have all offered insubstantial but persuasive connections, which I believe now need to be rethought; they have carried us into muddied, if exciting waters.

The heart of English

What are the central features of English that we must insist upon? If we cannot, or ought not, treat all language as our domain, what, essentially, should we be about? What would English look like if the kinds of criticisms I have put forward were heeded? Would it indeed be different from what goes on now – would there be some kinds of activity that would be omitted, altered, given a lower priority?

My own feeling is that all the elements we need are already largely with us – what is needed is a coherent synthesis that is based on sound apprehension of what those elements are, where their strengths lie, what their weaknesses are and how they relate to each other. A bare *list* of either the elements or the lesson activities would resemble an eclectic clutch of many of the existing ones. An examination of learning activities and their proper interrelation and interaction would reveal substantial differences from what they have often had in today's classrooms, under the influence of the linguistic view of language.

To construct a complete theory, even on the basis of highly developed but in the end inadequate predecessors, is a complex task doomed to some disappointment. It is anyway a task for collaboration, for reciprocating discussion. The criticisms that I have launched in this book are dependent on the existence of the theories which I have criticized. If my case turns out to be sound, this in turn will go towards a fuller expression.

What I am presenting is a case for reconsideration, not rejection. I want to suggest that we need to reconsider, or perhaps renew our understanding of, a few key points – what are the most important aspects of language, as far as we are concerned? What is the role of the teacher? What are the purposes of English? I shall attempt to sketch out some general statements and then see how those general statements affect English in practice, attempting to see unifying elements but yet preserve unique distinctiveness where appropriate.

In consideration of the first point, I want to insist that not all language is worth our attention – or on the other hand some kinds of human utterance are worth more than others, and of these, the one I see as characterizing English is that of *art-speech*,[132] in which I include the novel, poem, play, autobiography (whether created or received, silent or aloud, private or public). Literature is a vital part of it, but not all of it, since art-speech includes creation as well as reception.

The raw material of art-speech and of English is the personal experience of a human being, the living moment of existence. As Lawrence put it 'The business of art is to reveal the relation between man and his circumambient universe, at the living moment.'[133] Art is concerned with the meeting of public and private realms of experience, in an accessible middle ground, where our own uniqueness can be recognized alongside our human fellowship. When we make an utterance about our experience, we draw upon what it has been possible to say and the ways it has been possible to say it. It is in the potency of art-speech for helping us to recognize who we are that we place our hopes. We oscillate between absorbing meanings from others in books or in speech and formulating our own distinctive meanings, which are, in art-speech, simultaneously public and private. That is, the productive modes of language, talk and writing, are dependent on the receptive modes, reading and listening, which in turn need the active elements of talk and writing if they are to yield their full merit.

It is in this reciprocal relationship that there lies the truth of the unity of English. However, not all human language is equally capable of this empowering function. It is the *achievement* of art-speech that substantiates its claims to be given a special place. Poetry, the novel, drama, the short-story, autobiography are never wholly new starts, though they may feel like it. There exists an enormous human creation of great wealth and power that informs all that we say and offers us, properly approached as living utterance, an access of power.

It is this that has given literature, the core of art-speech, its significance. There is *no* comparable body of verbal human expression, in spite of the hopes of Peter Doughty; its value has nothing to do with whether or not it is in the expressive, transactional or poetic mode. The part of art-speech that is in literature has no value for itself, to be absorbed without effort. Its value exists only in recreative reading of this novel, that poem, that play (a performance based on a reading), and not all expressions of art-speech are equally valuable. It is unlikely that, for example, a child's expression, excellent and necessary as it might be, equals that of a mature artist. Also, much writing and drama is dead, circular, offering only a mechanical rehash of stereotype and cliché.

Art-speech bridges the gap between person and culture, allowing personal dimensions, indeed demanding them, while enriching the personal view with wider experience. T. S. Eliot called Donne 'expert beyond experience', a phrase which well describes the nature of what created art offers, the possibility of going beyond the confines of our own limited direct experience, to experience through the power of creative imagination more widely, more deeply, and to profit from that experience.

Art-speech is not the only meaningful part of language, but it is a vital, living, part that is in danger of being mislaid, as one among many. It is the business of English to deal with that part; or to put it the other way round, there must be a place in the life of the school for art-speech and we might call that part 'English'. There are other meaningful, civilizing parts of our language which show 'what fineness of life ordinary language makes possible, the fineness of the connexions between things by which we make a world in common'.[134] There are others that must have a place in schools, just as there are other, non-lingual orders of meaning that must be in schools, such as music and the plastic arts. But *we* must make art-speech our subject because it is so important to our children.

Around this vital core of 'art-speech', there will be clustered, as part of English, a number of other aspects of language which are instrumental or ancillary, taking their strength from art-speech, yet contributing essential features – of these the chief one I would include is that of discussion, which I will take up in more detail later.

To conclude, English is about those kinds of language which can be seen to be most successful at dealing with human experience as a felt reality. In these days of demands to educate for a practical world we must hang on to these essentials. Though he was speaking only for literature, Gordon Mason in a recent article makes a remark which may be adapted to the wider reference of art-speech: 'How is the sentient inner man to be educated – that part of the growing child which will so easily go by the board in favour of his becoming a useful and responsible member of society – unless English is assertively about literature and the independence of judgement and feeling?' [135]

Chapter 10

A teacher still

The good teacher tries to balance a sure sense of what there is to offer, what demands can be made on the pupil, with a strong awareness of the need for the pupil to take on his own learning. Without the former, the teacher will not be able to guide the child or persist in the face of difficulties; without the latter, the teacher is not likely to create chances, or to miss them, for the most powerful kind of learning. In practice, the good teacher has a combination of firmness and flexibility, a clear idea of what it is all for, demonstrates by example the qualities being sought, and has an ability to allow the children's contribution to affect the way the work is planned. It is at the moments of choice, whether to persist in the already chosen direction or to move aside at the child's angle, that the good teacher is shown.

However, at the root of the development in the theory of English teaching in the fifties and sixties was a view of learning which stressed the learner, rather than the teacher. More precisely it began by seeing learning as an active involvement by the learner in a step by step accretion onto an existing knowledge. Thus the conditions for learning were crucial to any successful education. Such a stress was salutary and of eminent pedigree and confirmed a loss of faith in the kind of teaching which delivered accepted facts, accepted judgements and indispensable skills to an empty pupil, filling him up. The survey of English teaching so far examined has demonstrated both a lively faith in the powers of the learner, given the right conditions, and a trenchant criticism of what has been usually called 'transmission' teaching among English teaching circles.[136]

I have not intended to question the laudable assumptions behind this approach to teaching. Children *will* learn better with an encouraging context; learning *is* a matter of connecting with what one knows; there *is* a prodigious power of creative construction at the call of the learning child, if he can be got to call; without such a personal investment, learning is fractured and temporary. Furthermore much that has gone on in schools has had no lasting benefit because it is not enjoyed, nor does it connect with the interests of the child.

These have been the guiding perceptions of English teaching of late and amount now to truisms. Frank Whitehead's *The Disappearing Dais*, John Dixon's *Growth through English*, the work of James Britton, Denys Thompson, they all have supported this move towards the child-centred approach, which has formed the basis for the criticisms of the influence of examinations, of knowledge 'about', of a certain kind of 'cultural heritage' teaching.

Starting from a faith that literature and reading appeal directly to the unique individual, the case has developed imperceptibly into a faith that the child's own responses are paramount, and sometimes, in confusion, that any response was sufficient. Thus the recent indifference to the claims of literature had a common ancestor with the persisting faith in its value. A failure to articulate precisely enough the claims of literature left an ambiguity which is now resolved into two 'sides'. The stress on the child's end has left unclear the nature of the contribution of the teacher – it certainly does not help in the reality of our schools to describe the teacher as support and adviser, because that kind of contribution is only appropriate some of the time, and it is ancillary to a larger purpose.

It has been a characteristic of recent years (I hope we are going beyond this now) for English teaching to be seen as a series of opposing choices – *either* knowledge *or* response, *either* discipline *or* enjoyment, *either* subject *or* individuality – so much so that calls for balance have not always been recognized as such. In particular, the stress on the learning individual has been seen as excluding the claims of the subject, a tradition or a culture. Yet there need be no such debilitating opposition. [137] Perhaps a consideration of some of the ideas of Michael Polanyi will clarify some of the issues, in the interrelationship of teacher, learner and subject.

Polanyi, a Hungarian by birth, was both a scientist and a philosopher of science. Of late many have come to see his ideas about 'knowing' as relevant to areas outside science, including language, education and the arts. His ideas present difficulties because of his terminology, yet they do merit close attention. He was concerned to develop a theory of knowing that would account for all that we learn. He saw knowing as a fusion between two elements, the personal and the objective. *All* knowing has an irreducible personal element, since all knowing is on the part of the knower. Any attempt to deny this, such as a belief in absolute objectivity, results in absurdity. Yet this knowing must also, for coherence, relate to ways of knowing that originate outside the knower.

The fusion of the personal and the objective was called by him 'personal knowledge'. He stressed that such knowledge was based on a tradition, which the knower could draw upon, for 'comprehension is neither an arbitrary act nor a passive experience but a responsible act'.[138] From this I understand him to imply that 'personal knowledge' is a creation of meaning that is a deliberate effort on the part of the knower, making use of what is known by others and responsible *to* others. It is an act of the individual knowingly in the light of the culture, the knowing, in which he lives.

If we refer this back to English teaching, this would mean that we seek to encourage the child's felt response and involvement with his English, but always within the context of an articulated culture. It is part of the teacher's role to insist upon this context; it is also part to invite a personal dimension on the part of the learner. It should be a characteristic of the work in English that it is *inviting*.

Whatever the form of knowing, for Polanyi it is an *art* 'which cannot be specified in detail' and 'which cannot be transmitted by prescription, since no prescription for it exists. It can be passed on only by example from master to apprentice'. Again, I interpret this as seeing all forms of knowing as like forms of wisdom, the fruits of experience, heart and mind in action. Knowing is something active, something which is shown in the actions of the person who knows. The terms 'master' and 'apprentice' present a difficulty, since it might be seen to imply a vessel-filling kind of learning, until we remember that there *must* be a personal dimension – 'neither an arbitrary act nor a passive experience'. Adopting for the moment the terms of Polanyi, but meaning by them for our present purposes teacher and learner, potent knowing seems to require a kind of *critical* submission to the knowing of another; there has to be an intermediary between learner and what is to be learnt (obviously the intermediary may be a book or other medium but Polanyi suggests that there has to be somewhere a human agency, a direct social transaction). The teacher is a person who knows both the subject and the learner and who *demonstrates* the knowledge in action. This places a great weight on the teacher for it means that the knowledge must be active in his life, if it is to be taken up by the child. The English teacher must demonstrate a lively curiosity and awareness of English as a force in his life. Reading and writing should be active; the teacher should be a considerate talker and a good listener.

The 'apprentice-ship' begins at the earliest moments of learning a language. 'All arts are learned by intelligently imitating the way they are practised by other persons in whom the learner places his confidence. To know a language is an art, carried on by tacit judgment and the practice of unspecifiable skills.' (We know of learning speech that it is not *simple* imitation, a mere parroting, but without an articulate adult about, a child does not speak, so we know some sort of mimesis is at work, though in a complex way.)

The confidence in the learner that we seek is a product of the teacher's own clarity of intention and considerate but firm approach, a product of the right kind of relationship.

Polanyi saw learning as part of a relationship, a communication of a particular kind between two persons: 'A true communication [learning] will take place if, and only if, [the] combined assumptions of authority and trust are in fact justified. . . . This kind of communication can be received only when one person places an exceptional degree of confidence in another.'

I suggest that it is the nature of learning English that the learning is two-way. The teacher must also be prepared to have a 'degree of confidence' in the pupils. Not only must the teacher deserve trust because of the sure ground of authority – knowing *and* caring; he must also learn, and learn from the pupil at times, if he is to sustain that trust, especially in English, where the diversity of experience gives everyone a moment of authority.

Yet even so, we must be clear as teachers how much we have to contribute to our pupils (and how much they want us to contribute). We are more experienced; we have pondered for longer; we have a degree of mastery in the arts we want to promote. That mastery should be continually renewed, so that we can convey the pleasurable fruits of that mastery. Because of what we offer, we ought to be able to insist on 'a degree of confidence' in us. In some situations, we are right to insist on such confidence *before* we have demonstrated the grounds on which it is to be based. We shall earn the trust later.

There will be some who see this submission as unhealthy, resulting in a slavish compulsive adoption of the ideas of another. This is always a danger, yet the teacher betrays the trust if he seeks to merely reproduce another in his own image. The knowing must always, if it is to be potent in the world, have a *personal* element, to which the individual can return. It must always, if it gives affiliation to the values of a community, transcend the influence of the person through whom it was transmitted, in turn submitting the ideas of the master or teacher to the scrutiny of those values. (Doesn't this bear out our experience that when we come to know well someone who is learned, impressive in their grasp and understanding, they turn out to acknowledge the debt they owe to some influential teacher or other?)

Polanyi sees knowing as in essence an obligatory submission, humbling but not humiliating. 'The effort of knowing is . . . guided by a sense of obligation towards the truth . . . by an effort to submit to reality. . . .

Since every act of personal knowing appreciates the coherence of certain particulars, it implies also submission to certain standards of coherence.' That is a recognition of the essential *discipline* of learning. Thus, the learner needs to read actively, with personal involvement, yet must seek the meaning that is there. Comprehension is a refining of our responses so that they are to a degree consonant with those of the writing (though not always what the writer intended). The teacher must be ready to insist on such attentiveness, to foster it and bring it to its full powers.

I suggest that the relationship that Polanyi offers between teacher and pupil, learner and culture, does offer us a valuable example that avoids the either/or fallacy. True, it does need careful study, if it is not to be taken simplistically, for the relationship should be convivial and mutually respectful.

Polanyi is also helpful when we turn to consider the nature of English, particularly if we think of its concern for 'art-speech', for he conceives knowing in the arts as in the form of 'an articulate framework' – that is in a form which has been used and found a powerful vehicle. A work of art (such as a play, a symphony or a poem) speaks out of a tradition, in a form that has been found meaningful. When we allow ourselves to experience a poem, we 'dwell' in it. Polanyi coined the word 'indwelling' to describe this inner experiencing.

'This indwelling can be consciously experienced' and 'The task of inducing an intelligent contemplation of music and dramatic art aims at enabling a person to surrender himself to works of art. This is neither to observe them nor to handle them, but to live in them. Thus the satisfaction of gaining intellectual control over the external world is linked to a satisfaction of gaining control over ourselves.'

I think English teachers would question the exclusion of 'observing' the work of art, but we would certainly echo the prime need to 'live' in a story, a poem or a play, to *experience* it before anything else; then we can observe what we have experienced. The bringing to life of a book or a poem is an active recreation, and the teacher plays a vital part, making available to children the life he has found. This life comes from an active, critical submission to the work and the recreation which is shared requires a similar approach. When the child reads alone, the bringing to life involves that same obligatory combination of interrogation and patience. The teacher is needed by many children to insist that such a possibility exists and its practice brings pleasure.

Polanyi offers some notes towards the unity that English has been seeking. The 'indwelling' is the personal response that recognizes what is there and is shaped by it. Experience is shaped also, by the 'articulate framework' which we adopt and to an extent adapt in the effort to reveal the truth. (This applies to the *production* of art as well as to the reception of it. Our children, in writing, in discussion, or in drama, can make use of this 'articulate framework'). The growth of the learner involves a 'from-to' relationship, a reciprocation between people, moving towards 'standards of coherence', which must also be present in the very learning situation.

Another associated feature of Polanyi's 'model' is that 'values' or 'standards' are given a place. Learning seeks an end in some way prefigured by the learned even when it takes the form of new knowledge. Lest it be thought that this leads to arid repetition, Polanyi points out that 'Every acceptance of authority is qualified by some measure of reaction to it or even against it'. That is, new thought or originality is born of apprenticeship to authority. It is here that Polanyi contrasts most strongly with the thinking of James Britton. Britton has seemed to reject all authority of the teacher in the learning in the school and has not sought to account for the role of values in that learning. However, in no way can Britton be blamed for the widespread and prolonged failure of the advocates of 'child-centred' education to face up to the actual difficulties of teaching and the need at times for insistence on the part of the teacher. Yet without a recognition of some of the realities in the pervading theory (such as the 'confrontation' of Pat D'Arcy) the teacher either allows purposeless drift or becomes a reactionary outcast.

Polanyi's approach offers a comprehensive and unifying view since it does have a place for the culture and a psychology of learning, which brings into balance the learner, the learning and the learned. It may even be possible to be realistic about the nature of teaching English today.

Chapter 11

The end of English

If we want to be dazzled with revelation, look at a mature tree in full blossom, a mature stallion in the full pride of spring. Look at a man or woman in the magnificence of their full-grown powers, not at a tubby infant.

Here is our responsibility, to see that this unformed thing shall come to its own final form and fullness, both physical and mental.

D. H. Lawrence

The end that I wish to see prefigured is more difficult to define than it was in the sixties. It is nevertheless true that education only makes sense as the prefiguration of a kind of adult life and a manifestation of the very quality of that life. The child's life is to be protected so that he can be childlike in due season, but what is essentially childlike can only be seen against what it is to be grown-up. Furthermore the very idea of 'childlike' presumes a normal and necessary move *from* it. It is a temporary, transitional stage, which must receive its due but only its due.

All children grow up in years, if they survive; all human beings do not reach the full flowering of their powers or the full entry into the community of humankind. Childhood and adolescence are perilous times when distorted viewpoints, fear and aggression play a substantial part. What we seek in education is the subsuming of these elements, common to us all, in a development towards a way of life that we call 'civilized'. It used to be possible, as Frank Whitehead did in 1966, to use this word without further comment; its meaning could be taken for granted. It seems it no longer is so.

What I mean here by 'civilized' includes a sustained talent for joy, curiosity and wonder, an unselfconscious awareness of the richness and beauty of our culture, a smell for living things, and a sense for 'those things that have gone dead'. It includes a taste for life and a recognition of the good life, a life of responsibility, sensitivity to others, and a due humility in the recognition of achievement. It includes a capacity to ponder, be critical, choose appropriate utterance. It involves a recognition of 'otherness' while sustaining a confidence in what one offers in one's life. It understands part at least of what it means to be human, what we have in common and what of infinite variety we can bear. It includes a capacity to feel deeply and think clearly, yet a readiness to accede to the dark mystery of existence.

110

In the search for such qualities as these, we are to an extent our own creators. We are also moulded by others, directly and indirectly. I suggest that in seeking this end, literature – poetry, fiction and drama – does have a vital role to play. Indeed I would at this point assert that it *is* central to English, for the reason that it is in itself characteristic of the very life we seek to foster. It is the characteristic of literature (and of art in general) to distinguish the quick from the dead; it is endlessly curious, and vital; it seeks to know self and what is not self; it is a created truth. But it exists only in this particular novel, that particular poem.

Literature and reading
The claims for the influence of literature have been extensive and often naïve. There is of course no inevitable influence on character merely because of contact; nor is it possible to show that those who study literature professionally are better people than those who do not. Anyone who claims so is a fool, for he is confusing the kind of effect that propagandists seek, manipulative and restrictive, fundamentally disrespectful, with that which the writer seeks, collaborative, reciprocating and profoundly respectful. Literature allows, indeed seeks, the personal response, that kind of attention that makes the book one's own creation and oneself part of the book. No book is the same for any two people, though any two honest readers will share a good deal. Whenever we think about the balance between individual understanding and shared meanings, the words of D. W. Harding should be remembered – they caution us against simplicity. There is, as he has pointed out, the problem of '. . . the relation between the writer's words and some other, non-literary, experience, whether his or his readers'. It is a dangerous area of interest, which comes and goes in fashion as one of two errors become more evident: the first, forgetting that the understanding of a poem (by the author or his readers) is an experience quite distinct from any other experience on which its creation and understanding may depend; the second, neglecting the requirement that the poem should be anchored closely enough in comprehended sense for the writer and the reader to be relating it to the same kind of other experience.'[139] The second, I suggest, has been our most recent neglect.

The kind of literature teaching that John Dixon rightly lampooned in his model of 'cultural heritage' seeks to impose a reading which is not personal and so it can be nothing. It seeks to manipulate the children. But on the other hand there is a kind of teaching which is party to that manipulation; it allows the reading of books that are manipulative, gone dead, without at the same time offering a critical framework in which to place them. We have a large industry seeking to manipulate (it sees it as 'satisfying the market'); there is now an adjunct to the educational publishing business which seeks to produce books of more than dubious quality, disrespectful to their readers to a degree, for teachers who fail to distinguish them from literature, perhaps because they see no right in themselves to offer any guidance or state any principled preference.

Recently, at a course for English teachers, I was attacked by a group for daring to suggest that the teacher had any right to select the kind of books that were available in the library or classroom library. It does not take much thought or experience to realize that selection there must be, since we cannot stock all books. No L.E.A. has enough funds and anyway books come low down on the list of priorities. If we have to select, we must decide on what criteria we select. The interesting thing about the argument with the other teachers was that they all in the end accepted that they *do* select, but usually on the basis of personal liking. Ironically they saw no manipulation in that approach, in which the child is at the mercy of one person's taste, but saw undue arrogance at work in the attempt to determine what kinds of books we *ought to* make available to children, which books we *ought to* share with them. Some relied on the supply of books from some superior source – a county librarian or the head of department.

I find depressing this refusal to accept the nature of the job of teacher – yet it is now very common. To assert that we *must* select, *must* consider restriction, *must* use judgment, is to be seen as power-mad. I suggest that a due sense of judgment is not only essential – it allows *wider* choice to our children in the end, because propaganda does drive out the very qualities we seek.

What in practical terms, does this imply for the teacher in the classroom, the head of English? Obviously the books available must stand up to scrutiny as 'Works of honesty, maturity, not books that pander or distort'. There must be a wide range of titles readily available in the classroom, school bookshop, and in the school library – poetry, novels, short stories and plays. Books must be readily available, of sufficient variety of theme, style and level of reading to be accessible to all children, if only they will give them a chance. There must be a general air of pleasure and reading time must be available in its most helpful form – sessions of silent reading.

I have watched children of other teachers (and my own) allowed to read in a hubbub of noise. This, I am sure, was fine for the fluent, 'hooked', readers – the others, more failing, with slender grasp on the meaning of the book and so more reluctant, these lost out every time, read little and experienced a confirmation of meaninglessness. So, I remain convinced that we must offer the silence of concentration and protect, insist on protecting, the tender growth of individual reading, which can only thrive on the child succeeding in drawing out a substantial portion of *meaning*. Living-in takes time.

It has become tempting to be over-modest about what books contribute to a developing child's mental and spiritual growth. Tempting also to believe that in an audio-visual world there is little future for the book; it might indeed by thought to be restrictive. However, the book remains a liberating force, even increasingly so. The Schools Council Report *Children and their Books*[140] made a number of encouraging, salutary, remarks, which I have referred to before. (See p. 83.)

Books do offer a range of meanings not available in any other medium, an accessibility and an achieved body of quality, which add up to an indispensable contribution to a growing child's development.

I am convinced also that we must share books with children, not so easy in a mixed ability class, but just as essential if we are to convey the power and enjoyment of reading to all. There are books which tell stories for us all. I suggest that we ought to read these, aloud, to all the class. I have found the following approach successful.

I read the book aloud, with each child in the class seeking to follow my reading in their own copy. I explain (this becomes expected) that I shall read through the whole book and that everyone will stay in the circle (we sit in a circle away from the desks) until I have read about one-third of the book. Then they have the option, if they prefer, of going into another corner or another room (the library nearby) while I continue to read aloud. I explain that they can read the book more *quickly* on their own and go onto their personal reading.

This method which is employed three times a year may seem restrictive, even mechanical. I have however found that it is very popular and that only avid readers leave the circle. The children look forward to the reading (and the interrupting discussion) and look back on it with enjoyment. They often remember the book read as among their favourites. The shared experience allows us to refer back to the books, and to the experiences in them, months later. Many of the children in the mixed-ability classes could not read, on their own, books of the length and complexity that I use. For example few of the simple readers have stories anything like as interesting as *Children of the Oregon Trail*, a class reader with the first or second year.

There is of course the problem of which books to choose. Some are rather light (*Midnight Fox*). Others are works of some merit, I feel, such that I as an adult ponder on the experience depicted in the same way as the child does. One in this category is *Carrie's War* by Nina Bawden, or

Philippa Pearce's collection of short stories *What the Neighbours Did*. They do explore honestly and offer in the reading an opportunity to become a little more understanding, a little wiser.

This method of sharing books (and enjoyment) has a number of intended goals. Many children repeatedly fail to finish a book, for various reasons, which becomes a habit. Reading a book to the class gives some experience of completion – once experienced it can be imagined again with another book. The feeling of the wholeness of a book is part of the comprehension of its parts.

I see reading at all levels as a matter of comprehension, from the very weakest child to the most able, and comprehension is a matter of meaning. For many children their problem with reading is its meaninglessness, because it is fragmented. A child who has a sense of the wholeness of a book has a key into meaningfulness. I have found Frank Smith enlightening on the subject of reading:

'We do not in fact attend to words; we attend to meanings. . . . Reading is not a passive activity – readers must make a substantial and active contribution if they are to make sense of print. . . . Reading is something that makes sense to the reader.'

More technically, 'The more non-visual information a reader has, the less visual information the reader needs.'[141]

Reading aloud to children offers the following essential 'non-visual' information to a child that (1) reading is meaningful (2) reading is enjoyable (3) reading is sharable (4) whole books have whole meanings (greater than the parts) (5) it is possible to finish a book (6) difficulties, such as less dramatic parts, are surmountable.

In the process of reading aloud, we are 'trusting the tale' (or the poem) to do its work, though we as the vocal medium are necessary to it. At other times, to stimulate the kind of thinking attentiveness that enables the reader to absorb the meaning of a work of literature, we might employ some of the techniques described by John Dixon, Leslie Stratta and Andrew Wilkinson in their book *Patterns of Language* – such as the children producing dramatic readings, radio versions, documentaries based on part of a novel. These are all ways of encouraging active reading, though they do have dangers of leading away too easily from the meaning of the original into some personal exploration.

Narrative and poetry are available as sources of patterned, meaningful experience and must be approached as such. A vital factor here is the talk that flows around a shared reading, in which words are weighed, actions pondered, persons judged. There is a discipline to the best talk of this kind, since it is subjected to controls by the participants. The talk also contributes a discipline. All the time it returns to the people, places, actions of the book by attending to the words – the more involved the discussion, the more attentive the re-reading. Of course the discussion will move away into personal experience, which sometimes will make its own sufficient point. But often it is on the return to the book that the experience related is put into perspective for the group. Hopefully also the direct experience has been brought to bear on the book (or poem) making it more personally alive.

I have used the word 'discipline' in describing work around a book, because I believe that if the real value of literature, talk, writing or listening is to be gained, we must accord due weight to the particular qualities of the mode and of the matter. A book is to be pondered and to be understood; it is not enough to extract a section as a stimulus for its spin-off, for that is to under-value what is distinctively offered – a coherent, perspective creation of a world. Reading may lead to talk or to writing, but its own strengths must be retained.

The critical, evaluative faculty is present in the very earliest responses and this should be fostered in the talk and writing on books; not that there should be a demand too early that children can sum up whole books with acumen. Rather it is parts of books, the detail of the whole, which they should be encouraged to weigh and discuss from an experience of the whole. For example at the upper junior/lower secondary level, after a reading of *Fresh* by Philippa Pearce, we can raise for discussion the actions and motives of the older boy who covets the fresh-water mussel, the atmosphere of the river and its part in the story, the enigmatic reaction of the older boy to the younger one's effusive thanks for keeping the mussel alive. . . . 'Don't thank me.' [142]

The best critical work is through talk and it leads to deeper understanding – of the book and of experience – of 'life', as we used to say with easy certainty. It also, I believe, deepens enjoyment if it is done tactfully.

The question of understanding is taxing. Publishers are again, I notice, producing books of passages with questions which are supposed to develop the faculty of 'comprehension'. I had thought that such an approach was discredited long ago. The passages have no context and usually after being slit off from the parent plant, precious little life. They are usually too short to develop any life of their own. Of course, publishers never stopped producing such books – but surely no conscientious teacher can mount any serious case for them – they are intended for teachers who want to deepen understanding in the pupils and do not know how to go about it any other way. (I am being charitable in ignoring the connexion with examinations, where ten questions on a passage remains a very popular means of testing; what is examined, that shall we teach, and in the same way.)

However, notwithstanding this false friend, there remains the problem of how to empower a child to read progressively more deeply. English teachers have for some time believed that a child who reads is at the same time increasing in the power to understand and nothing else needs to be done. Where we have invested in a vast range of individual readers, we send the children off to read them, confident in their power. I have already claimed such a power in literature, if it be allowed to do its work. The problem is that reading as I see it is an active, interrogative process, not a soporific, and the habit of active reading must be caught or taught for most of our children (a precious few will devour books and construct meaning on their own).

Recently such techniques as are described in *Patterns of Language* and *Reading Development and Extension*[143] have been taken to offer a way forward. Undoubtedly we need to consider them as part of our teaching equipment, since the methods advocated in both books focus attention on what is read, either prospectively or retrospectively. (Walker sees understanding as an *anticipatory* feature of reading; Dixon, Stratta, and Wilkinson offer approaches which demand a reconsideration, a rereading in the light of a new demand, such as a changed viewpoint or a visual presentation.) Valuable as they are the limitation of these methods is this: they are essentially formal, in that they are only usable in an institutional setting – the school or the college. They cannot be transferred to the single reader, reading for his own purposes outside the confines of the teacher-learner relationship. They demand the presence of someone who knows the book or the passage well enough to select an appropriate method of treatment; or they demand a group to read with.

If these methods do enhance reading, boost comprehension, they do not offer a style of reading that can be carried over into adult life, whereas, I suggest, a dialogue about books, together with shared readings, which indicate *how to* read, can be absorbed, taken into the pupil as a technique. (As the centre of a dialogue about books, a record of a pupil's reading provides very useful *concrete* subjects for regular discussion.)

It should be obvious that *poetry* cannot be allowed to slip out of our lessons, as it will so easily do. If our intentions are as I have suggested they ought to be, then poetry must take up its vital role. Children should hear and read a lot of poetry, preferably from a range of sources, not just the one anthology in stock. It should be read with vigour, aloud and for interest, for if it does not interest, it is nothing. Many English teachers, because of the difficulty and the predictable resistance from pupils (*where* does it come from?), have found themselves leaving it out.

As a teacher, I recognize the difficulties and I would not want to pretend that poetry is easy to present to today's pupils. No teacher who dislikes or is indifferent to poetry should teach it. Yet I feel that not to teach poetry must be felt as a sad omission, something to grieve over and feel guilty about – not a matter of indifference.

In all the work with books, reading, literature, we can rely on the evidence that despite the difficulties we can have an effect. English departments that believe they can encourage reading for enjoyment do succeed. English teachers who believe in and work hard at the possibilities of enhancing a pupil's power of reading do succeed. We can make few more vital contributions.

Talk, Listening and Drama

Schools are full of talk. The hubbub heard by the visitor is all talk of one kind or another. Most of us would admit that some of it at least is not very productive. Some is decidedly counter-productive. Yet if talking goes on throughout the day, little of it is seen by the school as important to the learning of the pupils, particularly the talk of the pupils. In this respect the situation has not changed greatly since Andrew Wilkinson wrote in *Spoken English* [144] 'The spoken language in England has been shamefully neglected'. This might now be surprising in the light of the immense efforts made to develop work in this sphere. English departments are in this respect distinctive. The work on 'oracy' has led to talk being admitted into the canon with gusto, sometimes with outrageous expectations, and exaggerated claims. *Spoken English* was very much a mixture, containing very useful ideas and a sound case for a new consideration for talk, alongside some special pleading arising out of the need to make that case. At times, the book contained simplistic claims which if taken seriously would lead to inflated confidence in the power of speech. For example 'Speech and personality are one', or 'If literacy is important, oracy is more so'.

These remarks are similar to those in the sixties about literature – they stress the importance of what is advocated without relating it to the other aspects of language and culture. Yet *Spoken English* for its part contained some very careful formulations as well as these few unbalanced ones. Teachers of English have been more persuaded by the exciting assertions than by the remarks calling for careful working out of implications. For example in writing of the school's respect for silence, Andrew Wilkinson wrote 'Discrimination is all' – that is silence is good in some situations, bad in others. The same could be said for talk; even more, there needs to be discrimination in the *kinds* of talk employed and taught.

The book did not always discriminate itself, as when Alan Davies (tongue in cheek?) suggests that children in schools might be helped to use registers unknown to them, such as the register of Youth Employment Officers! There was at bottom an over-inclusiveness such as we have seen from other advocates of language in education, a readiness to include *all* kinds of speech. Andrew Wilkinson wrote 'The technique of listening is to be sharpened on the spoken language itself in *all* its manifestations'. (My italics.) Surely not! Wasn't this a plea for extending the range inflating itself beyond measure? Do we want to sharpen children's listening on teacher's invective, assembly sermons, parental arguments?

However, after this carping, it must be said that there remain many elements in the book which, if read more carefully in the years since its publication, might have avoided the position we have got ourselves into with talk in schools. The situation now seems to be one where some teachers have lost confidence in the power of talk in their English lessons because they started out with inflated expectations. Others have failed to differentiate between the kinds of talk which we should encourage and those to discourage (or be indifferent to); just because there is *talk* does not mean something valuable is happening. When one looks now for help with understanding the relation of talk to writing or to reading, one finds little convincing help. Yet in 1965 *Spoken English* already defined the problem. 'The task ahead is to define [oracy] in terms of particular skills and attainments, for different ages, groups, circumstances; to discover the best methods of teaching it; to bring it into synthesis with other work, especially that designed to promote literacy.' We are in English teaching little further on in defining it.

Andrew Wilkinson in particular made some very important points in considering talk. 'The *quality* of language experience is crucial; quantity, though necessary, is not enough. The wrong language experience may result in a culturally induced backwardness.' The need for selection is there, yet many English teachers still wallow in an undifferentiated morass of talk which is vaguely felt to be going somewhere, yet unable to convince even themselves of its point.

The way forward, a dangerous one if followed without discrimination, was outlined by Wilkinson: 'literacy and oracy must go hand in hand, supplementing and vitalizing each other'.

It is this kind of involvement that I seek in the talk in class about what is read. But each element must in that flow be used with discipline so that it contributes what it can do best and does not usurp a role it can not perform. Talk is exploratory, tentative, even when assertive. It can retract, reform, adjust easily. Thus personal experience lends itself well to being talked about, allowing anecdote which is shaped in the telling, understood in the discussion. Talk implies listening and response, and talk about experience calls for response *from* the listeners, response *to* the listeners, reformulation. Talk is a modulating form of expression, a collaborative development, when it is working properly (it does not always do so, it needs to be said). Talk can bring into connexion the experience on the page and the experience we live so that we understand them both, and their differences. It cannot do what reading and writing can do in their own distinctiveness, and it will fail if it tries. For example talk cannot have the stamina nor the developed coherence of writing. Talk requires a listener, and a good listener encourages good talk. In all the talk that we encourage, we are encouraging listening; deaf ears restrain articulacy.

What kinds of talk?
There are I suggest some kinds of talk we can happily promote, because they reflect our search for a mature, civilized way of life; they demonstrate it in action; most of them are parts of the *art-speech* that I have claimed as the staple of English. They are:
—discussion and story-telling
—collaborative planning
—presentation
—role-playing and drama.

DISCUSSION AND STORY-TELLING
I see talk about experiences as dependent on a reciprocal relationship between people who respect each other's viewpoint, but seek to arrive at the most truthful one. In developing this rational mode of speech the teacher is very important. Some children experience discussion at home and so accept the rules (discussion is rule-governed, like all potent language skills); many, the majority, need to experience it before they can learn how, slowly and sometimes frustratingly. The teacher is the source of that experience, but not a source that should forget how to listen and learn from the young.

Of late we have been made aware of the way the teacher tends to dominate discussion ('discussion is really listening to teacher') and we must beware of this. Nevertheless we should neither accept this as inevitable nor believe that we must pull out and leave the children to find their own way. Many children flounder in distressing frustration if left to their own devices in discussion, though they must be allowed at times to develop their own teacher-free exchanges. The teacher, if he can avoid an easy domination, can offer an example of good listener, enjoying the stories and comments of others, weighing them and pointing out a strength or, more carefully, a weakness in a point. It is respect for the child not contempt which suggests that at times we might treat their utterances as worth sufficiently serious consideration that we mount a counter-argument. As Roger Harcourt has put it: 'The chance to have his opinions and feelings rubbed against those of the teacher is potentially one of the most educative things that can happen to the student.'[145]

We must give the child room in discussion, room to make mistakes and follow false trails so that he might discover, but we must also be firm when those trails are too destructive of the respect for others or the truth as we can best realize it. This protective restraint is most important for the least articulate and for the most aggressive. As usual it is the weakest who suffer in an unrestrained classroom.

I have already indicated that most work to develop comprehension should be approached through talk about what has been or is about to be read. Such discussion attends to concrete detail, and should be carried on throughout the school years. As children get older they usually want to deal in more abstract subjects. Very energetic arguments can be experienced, enjoyed by all, yet we must remember always that abstractions are avoiding thought if they are not rooted in particulars. The role of the teacher here might be to bring back such discussion to earth by questions of detail. In this respect, the move of talk to generalization is part of a maturing child's development – the same safeguards need to be applied as in reading and writing – generalizations must be rooted in particulars, or only shallowness will result.

An essential element of discussion is *evaluation*, when we weigh what we are discussing, whether it be a poem, an anecdote from a class member, a statement of opinion. Throughout the school years, there should be a lot of *story-telling* between members of a class. At first it will be merely a sequence, drawn out by a short story or what the last person has said; the exchange of personal experience in an atmosphere of enjoyment and attention. Increasingly the stories will show growing perspective, with an evaluative commentary from the story-teller, more explicit than it would be in the same story written. This exchange of personal experience relates of course to literature, though it is no substitute; it is a basis for comparison, for adding on to what one knows. It is a preparation for writing, though writing will have a more careful and finished relation between the elements. It is related to drama, handling some of the experiences which can be explored in role-play.

PLANNING

A good deal of work in English should be in groups, whether it be, for example, a presentation of a playlet, mounting a display of writing, taping a discussion, or creating an anthology of favourite poems. In this work there will need to be co-operation, through talking. Such talk, if it avoids violence, is successful to some degree, yet it is rather more instrumental than is discussion. It is a means to an end – the presentation or whatever. It demonstrates our sharing of the world, should be respectful, should involve much listening and is the kind of talk that should be encouraged everywhere in the school. It is not specifically the province of English, but part of the whole aim of education. The teacher will play a major role in fostering such co-operative talk, and in discouraging wrangling, personal abuse, the resort to fisticuffs.

PRESENTATION

A lot of the oral work in English will be presented to others, the class, the school, visitors, other classes, other schools. This provides both a powerful stimulus to careful, disciplined work and an alternative to the teacher as audience. A reading, a dramatization, a tape, a documentary – the list is endless as to what can be done. The best work of this kind will raise the quality of expression above the everyday and will be a form of art. Indeed, that should be the aim, so that the children experience satisfaction and benefit from the shared meaning of the presentation.

ROLE-PLAYING AND DRAMA

It is here that English merges into drama but returns to art-speech. A child benefits from a playful improvised exploration of some other person's life or behaviour in some interacting people. It is an acted story, in which the acting stimulates and feeds off the imagination. We used to, I think, too easily believe that some kind of emotional involvement occurred in drama, releasing catharsis and understanding of others. Though we now accept that the mind must be involved in drama, not solely emotion, it is too frequently accepted that drama's claims have proved to be disappointing. Beneath the naïvety of the sixties, there remains a good deal of truth, even after the exaggerations are stripped away. Good drama does contribute development that we ought to be after, a disciplined, balanced investigation of otherness, an enjoyment of vicarious experience, which is both imaginative and critical, since drama requires a great deal of discussion before and after, refining and deepening the understanding and feel of the experience, relating it to other experience, and to literature.

The drama does not need always to be improvised. The scripted play brings literature and dramatic work together. There is a problem of supply, especially for younger children. There is, however, more now than there was, and it can be a very enjoyable, rewarding experience to read a play with a class, whether or not it is fully dramatized. It is a very disciplined kind of collaboration. The reading itself demands attentiveness and necessitates discussion all along the way. If we are lucky we can find scripts in which the dialogue, the words, matter, and in much the same way as a good story.

A good play demands the life of dramatization. A proper approach is to bring out the meaning on the page into a realized actuality; an improper one is to merely use the play as a starting-point for improvisation, for that is to miss the possibilities.

The play written by children is a middle station, rarely literature in its own right, but often with some achievement in it sufficient to base some further work on it, usually presentation. What children can rarely create is a play in which the words themselves create complex meanings, such as they can sometimes do more successfully in short dialogue in a story. One way is to create a play using the actual dialogue from a reader. Otherwise few of the children's plays will contain 'memorable words in memorable order'. It is a characteristic of art-speech, the kind of language we ought to be concerning ourselves with, that it is not interchangeable with another selection of words. A book worth reading, a good story from a child, the words of a play that is memorable, have this in common, though the differences in quality might be marked. Drama can also be preparatory to a poem, a story or to writing. It can, in improvisation, loosen the pondering faculty, suggest possibilities, alternatives, by its playful nature, that are unthreatening, can be quickly refined or abandoned, or more hopefully can set up fruitful lines of development.

I remain convinced that drama has a unique and necessary contribution to English and to an increasing mastery of English, without needing to stray into the field of psychotherapy. It is another aspect of English that has become optional, a matter of personal fad, picked up by enthusiasts or comfortably ignored by those who have no training. I believe drama should not be taught by someone who is very reluctant, any more than poetry should be, but anyone who sets out to teach English conscientiously and well ought to have very good reasons if drama is not to contribute. It is not an extra, but an essential, contributing something unique in its own right.

Nevertheless it has suffered from inflation. Drama should be there to contribute what it can do best, not to take over. It should be in essence an accession of control over the language, a form of creation; it has impact, immediacy, but is evanescent unless it is centred on a text.

It is a point I cannot resolve, as to whether mime has a substantial part to play in English. Its value I accept whole-heartedly and if it is not being handled elsewhere, then I would want it done in English. But is that its rightful place? If English is to do with words, where comes mime? On the other hand if English is to do with personal experience, then mime has a place. Whatever our decision, we must be clear *why* it is in or out and what part it is to play in the development of English. Acceptance of its value alone is not enough, otherwise I would include for example drawing, reading history, singing, all arguably humanizing. Some would say that this shows the absurdity of subject boundaries, which it does; to ignore the problem is to court just that incoherence that I have detected in our present developments. What is certain is that human creativity will not fit *neatly* into any category system, whether it be subjects or disciplines. There is a great deal that I wish well elsewhere in the life of the school, without insisting it is part of English; I would expect to collaborate with these other kindred spirits, without absorbing them or being absorbed.

Where improvised drama is used to explore a theme in a novel or the experience behind a poem, it is in a sense introductory to an approach to the novel's own words, not an equal or an exchangeable substitute. (At least, I hope we deal with books that are good enough for that to be true.) It is at the interaction between drama and literature, or talk and literature, that there is the greatest danger of missing what literature has to offer; it is there that great care must be employed.

Writing

What role does writing play in the whole subject English? What *kinds* of writing should we seek to develop in our pupils? What is the relationship of that writing to the other aspects already discussed, reading, talk and drama?

Just as in the other modes, we are not, cannot be, concerned with *all* writing, though of late, under the influence of the Bullock Report and the London Institute, it has been difficult for English teachers not to be concerned in looking at the way writing is used in content subjects. Yet we do have a major task of our own which is the development of ways of writing essentially related to the reading in English. There has been, since the sixties, a loss of enthusiasm for our children's powers of writing creatively, in narrative or poetic form. Under the influence of such writers as David Holbrook there was then a surge of work of great freshness and power. Holbrook asserted the essential creativity of each human being and the need for that creativity to be exercised. As the motto of *English for Maturity* he quoted Charles Ives, the American composer: 'Every normal man – that is, every uncivilized or civilized human being not of defective mentality, moral sense, etc, has, in some degree, creative insight . . . and an interest, desire and ability to express it.'[146]

Holbrook claimed that 'at the centre of education there needs to be that pleasure which propagates sympathy and is the basis of civilization: the pleasure of organizing experience in art.'

That is, in what came to be called 'creative' or 'imaginative' writing, which is now, like much else that blossomed in the sixties, discredited to the extent of raising a sneer. I believe that, though there have been, as in drama, excessive claims made for such writing (not least by Holbrook himself in his later books) for the promotion of psychic wholeness by the writing of story and poem, there is an essential place in our work for the stimulation and encouragement of the creative spirit. When English teachers lose heart in that, they fall in danger of losing heart in the whole enterprise. More mundane writing there must be; attention to technical conventions there must be; but the life in writing so far as English is concerned is to be found in art-speech.

Where we might be mistaken is in supposing that creativity is merely to be loosed upon the world. As Holbrook pointed out, creation requires control. It is not to be confused with effusiveness and self-indulgence. It needs a discipline just as much as the other aspects of English. It needs to be led, not by slavish adoption of 'models' (John Dixon saw this as a danger in 'cultural heritage' teaching) but by wide reading of honest writers and by teachers who read, write themselves, read the pupil's work with sympathy. Where a pupil can do better, he should be shown how to move forward to greater control. Guidance should always be offered in terms of making the meaning clear; the teacher is a necessary control. Any teacher who sees control here as suppression or interference is condemning most children to flounder in frustration. Again, a child must be allowed room to make his own movements in a controlled setting, seeking to tell stories, create poems, narrate experiences (autobiography is created) which explore the nature of living.

This kind of writing seeks just those ways of living I have called 'civilized'; indeed, they exemplify them, and they show them in action. Writing in this way is potent in working at the interface of experience, the living moment. As the child's powers develop, there emerges an enlarged perspective, which yet maintains a *personal* dimension. The individual seeks meaning by way of public meanings. No more than drama is it an expression solely of emotion. It requires judgment, a critical approach to one's own utterance, that is essential to development.

There are some kinds of experience that mould us, that echo through our lives. Literature may foreshadow them before they happen to us – we are perpetually curious, even afraid, of their coming. Injustice and punishment; loneliness, joy and loss; birth, death and love; the life of the family, its tensions and serenities; success and failure; kindness, nobility, courage, and the darker side of man; mortality, pain and fear; the mystery of living things; the seasons; the unnameable and the inexplicable; mirth, merriment, and ecstasy.

Of course, literature is 'about' these, and so should be much of the writing of children, under the guidance of the teacher and the reading that is experienced together. It is these central human experiences that lie beneath all that we do, or should do, for much that we do is very trivial by comparison. These experiences need not be handled with solemnity – humour is a human way to understanding and coping, and children have a healthy bubbling humour that yet conceals a fascination with the 'eternal verities'.

J. H. Walsh identified some of the more fertile kinds of experience for children's writing. He characterized the writing as 'those highly personal descriptions of experience in which the writer reveals not only a set of circumstances but also his feelings, his perceptions and his manner of involvement. As compared with ordinary reports and accounts they revolve more around the writer's self, they have greater intensity and they contain more of what might be called the substance of living.'[147]

The kinds of experience he had in mind were described as 'all those events in the children's lives which, because they are accompanied by emotion and strong feeling, are lived with the sort of intensity that facilitates their recapture in words', such as private festivals, visits to agreeable relatives, making of new friends, quarrels, reconciliations, homecomings, 'first days', hideouts and secret resorts, sudden snow.

Children have many interesting experiences to relate in writing (often stimulated by oral story-telling first), yet they also often require to be encouraged to think they are interesting *enough*. The teacher plays a vital part in helping the children to recognize what they have to offer, which is why the most important kind of 'marking' is a comment on what is *meant*. The teacher can help the child to recognize himself through his writing.

They are also, I repeat, interested in experiences to come and here literature encourages the child to 'think on these things'. As J. H. Walsh wrote about the connexion between reading and writing: '. . . it [writing] surely ought to do what the reading of good fiction in effect does do – provide a space in which [the child] can move about freely, experimenting with new emotions and situations, and thus preparing himself for the shocks and stresses (anticipating, too, the delights) of later life. The reading of good fiction does this; and the writing of stories can do it too especially when it is undertaken under the influence of good fiction previously read.'

There is still a lot of good personal and imaginative children's writing produced, perhaps more quietly, but nevertheless there. It is sometimes trapped in its own limitations, particularly the cathartic distortions of adolescence. It is not to be confused with mature writing, usually, but we have been right to see the child-writer as having the same purposes as the mature writer. There are essential differences, such that children's writing, 'the literature of the classroom' cannot take the place of mature work. (Nevertheless it does have a use as preparatory or ancillary to literature.)

In the Spring 1978 edition of *English in Education* Robert Protherough surveyed in an article[148] the rise and demise of the 'creative writing movement'. Protherough, in a very careful analysis, set out to write an epitaph, but in the event, salvaged what I would like to see retained. The criticisms (and thus warnings) were that teachers in the 'movement' had used a stimulus/response approach to writing that was essentially 'mechanistic' – 'passive children waiting to be "fed" with new experience'.

'The focus was on feeling rather than on writing: the need not only to experience but communicate that experience to somebody else in words.' That is, the writing lacked discipline, control, a public dimension. As a result of these fundamental weaknesses it became difficult to see any role for criticism, either from the writer's own judgment or from the teacher, in the same way that we might not feel able to criticize an infant's finger painting. Compare for example Peter Abbs on creative writing in *English for Diversity* 'Let us not worry over details of formal correctness, nor let us worry about assessing it.'[149]

Protherough made an important distinction '. . . the writer's raw material isn't either as immediate or as exclusively aesthetic as paint: it is the language in which we exchange information, complain about the weather, order a meal, call to the dog, shout at the children. The hearer, the reader, is an essential part of the activity, and the reader's response in many, perhaps most, classroom situations has to be presented by the teacher. How effective? how clear? fluent? well-organized? vivid? authentic? and so on are literary questions that have to be asked. Encouragement is vital, but are we putting so much stress on encouragement that we become afraid of making *demands*?' Just so.

He noted the frequent 'emphasis on brief, personal forms' to the exclusion of developed forms that require stamina, extended connexion, coherence over a range of material, or those that have specific conventions, such as the short story or the play.

After these well justified criticisms, Robert Protherough moved on to their implications. He still felt able to salvage the main elements. 'The emphasis on personal imaginative writing needs to be maintained and extended. . . . Despite the reservations mentioned, there *is* a place for stimulus/response techniques, properly handled; they can enliven, create a desire to express.'

I would add that we must beware of any obsessive use of one kind of stimulus; we should be ready to talk, improvise, read, tape, show film, in order to excite and intrigue our children in experience and its exploration. We can distinguish those kinds of writing where we seek impact and response that is 'off the top of one's head' and that which arises from a more digestive, ruminatory origin.

Protherough mentioned in his article a survey of how, according to their teachers, pupils were stimulated to their best writing. His conclusion provides a thought-provoking contrast with John Dixon's criticism of teaching by models.

'Virtually all [the teachers] have said it was the use of a literary model in one form or another' that provoked the best writing. Protherough asked 'Is this surprising?' implying a warm relationship between children's writing and literature, between receptive and productive modes, between the cultural creation that can be brought to the child and the creation of meaning that the child is involved in. We will recall Polanyi's 'articulate framework'.

One of the mistakes in the 'movement' that Robert Protherough did point out can be brought in here. The usual use of a poem, a part of a novel or even a film was to rely on a very short, sharp impact which was required almost immediately to be turned into writing. The material of the stimulus was not given any careful thought, not looked at in its own terms. In this way chances were repeatedly lost to inform the writing of the children with the discipline and complexity, the attention to the experience and to the task of mastering it in words or picture. The very haste of the injunction to write insisted on writing that was fresh, striking at times, but limited – more limited than it need have been. It also had a destructive effect on the attention to reading elsewhere in English. It was all part of an over-emphasis on feeling. As Protherough wrote: 'The creative operation needs to be balanced by the critical: the stimulated writing is to be seen *not* as the end-product, but as a stage in a process.'

That process is two-dimensional. Firstly it is a continuing attempt between teacher and pupil, to master the experience. Secondly, the process is related to the whole of the pupil's work in English. The first involves an understanding of how this kind of writing lays a foundation for, leads on to, writing that is more distanced, cooler, concerned with greater abstraction and generalization. The second requires the kind of grasp of a child's incremental development that demands keeping profiles on each child's progress according to precise criteria. There is a lot of work to be done there.

The move outwards in English writing into more abstract modes does not mean that at any time the personal and imaginative ones are superseded. Rather that the new ones develop very much on the basis of the personal involvement with experience, never get too far away from them, or abstraction becomes rootless and thus meaningless. The kind of critical writing about literature or the mass media that we want to encourage as the child grows older should always, for its own good, be related to direct and vicarious experience that is both felt and 'placed'. Where this is not so we shall encounter writing that offers another's opinion as one's own, an opinion that gets in the way of understanding, rather than offering perspective.

At no time do we outgrow the value of being creative, of exploring in the imaginative or personal modes the experience of living. It is absurd that university English departments who presumably stand for the primacy of literature as a symbolic mediation of experience should deny the value of actually writing ourselves. Some go even further and have asserted that there is no place for imaginative writing after sixteen, so that any involvement of such writing at sixth form level or in the proposed N & F syllabuses (see the N.A.T.E. proposals) is regarded by these guardians of literature as a weakness. Yet if we believe in the value of the creative and created achievement of the imagination in literature, surely we must also believe in the value of its active contribution in our lives.

The experience of the child and the world outside the classroom

There are three aspects of English that become clearer if we accept the crucial, characterizing role of 'art-speech'. In the sixties a great deal of words were devoted to counter the common belief that dialect or colloquial speech was 'wrong'. There had been a lot of effort by schools to eradicate, at least during lessons, the local speech and 'encourage' what was often called 'bilingualism' – the ability to speak 'properly' when required while yet speaking in the local way at home or among friends.

Quite rightly, students of language pointed out the misguided basis for these ideas, yet many schools, and many English teachers see 'proper' English as their subject. I suggest that this belief might have been countered more effectively had the linguists not, by their insistence that all languages, all dialects, are equal, confused social status with linguistic power. To say that all language is equally powerful is to go beyond all knowledge and all sense. What does seem to be within knowledge to say is that all the dialects and colloquial forms of English seem to be very rich, richer than many a teacher from the outside realizes. All local forms of English are capable of expressing civilized relationships, though many do not easily convert into written forms. Most literature in English can be taken and read with the local accent without destruction; much writing is enriched by a degree of local phrasing. It is in oral work that pronunciation has seemed a sad failure, yet it is the spoken form of local English that is usually the richest. I believe we English teachers should be drawing on this local richness, because it is in the speech that much of the life of the people resides. The experiences of importance to the children are couched in local words, local phrases, local pronunciation. To place a taboo on them is to exclude much of the valuable life of the child from the educational transaction. (Of course many schools still do that effectively.) Let me distinguish – I do not mean that we should ask for an exaggerated, self-conscious use of local dialect. We should be ready to draw on the best that is there in accepting local life in language, while discouraging any expression that is ineffective, or unsuccessful, just as we would with any other kind of speech. To help children to realize the possible social disadvantages of a particular way of speaking is not the same as being a dedicated agent in the inquisitorial eradication of that way in our pupils. We are already efficient enough in schools in persuading our pupils that education is not for them; to deny them utterance is to deny them the chance to connect the life of the classroom with the life they live outside.

Another aspect of English that generates a good deal of heat and not much light is that collection of conventions in writing that we call 'spelling' and 'punctuation'. Of course children do need to master these – we do them a disservice if we let them ignore them. But we must be clear about the reasons. The major one is to do with social respect. Employers and others do find it easy to recognize failure here – and our children should not fall foul of criticism which we can help them to avoid. Certainly we should not visit our own lack of interest on our pupils and send them as our unsuspecting ambassadors into the world. Even so, we should preserve some perspective. The functions of spelling and punctuation are partly to aid communication, partly to satisfy printers and proof-readers, and partly to satisfy small minds or small-mindedness. It is the first that justifies our attention, though our children should be aware of the others. Our major concern in writing is with *meaning* – without that there is no purpose in the conventions. Our concern in English is no greater with these conventions than any other subject in which writing is done, except that it is practical to put it with us. There really is not much point in teachers of other subjects bewailing the bad spelling of pupils and then saying that they are too busy to see to it themselves. There are ways, some important, in which we can be said to 'serve' the rest of the curriculum – this seems to be one of the least important ways.

The third aspect that becomes clearer is the relationship of English with the popular forms of entertainment, TV, pop radio, the mass press and so on. I have said we cannot be indifferent, because the very stuff that they concern themselves with – words to handle experience – is what we are concerned with. There has been a staggering change in the attitude of English teachers towards the mass media since the sixties. Then we felt (as Denys Thompson felt) that we had to counteract this hostile world's influence on our children by all out assault and criticism (see *Discrimination and Popular Culture*[150]). Now it seems the norm that there is *no* strong resistance, rather a compliance, so that if the mass media are treated it is either with a degree of shared enjoyment or a sociological, superficial course in techniques.

The combative stance of the sixties has been felt to have failed, yet that does not mean that we should not see damaging influence now and be sorry for the effects. Nor that we should not still seek to counter the *harmful* influences. The mass media remain essentially reductive – they have not improved, except in their ability to persuade larger and larger numbers to choose between fewer and fewer things (whether products, programmes, or points of view), and we must try to help children to see through the spurious, the destructive, the shallow, the dishonest. If we leave them to find their own way we could be condemning them to be manipulated or to be cynical, for without something of quality to which to turn, the shrewd and honest mind which sees through the manipulation of the mass media is shorn of a sense of value, and thus of hope.

The television cops and robbers serial deals with the same experience that we do, yet it usually simplifies, distorts, titillates. We cannot ignore it. Yet neither should we merely criticize it, or worse still, criticize our pupils for watching it. The most fruitful approach is by encouraging in discussion a discriminating habit of thought, by helping a child to develop a set of criteria that sees the good as well as the bad. There are good qualities in some popular media, especially on television or in film. We should encourage children to see the good and to widen their range from among what is available.

We should also see to it that we offer experience in art that has quality and try to help (it goes without saying) children to recognize that quality. A lot that is now on offer to 'the reluctant reader' is *worse* than that offered by the mass media.

It is not, however, our main purpose in English to be 'anti' anything. It is to be *for* the good things in life and in literature, *for* the good things in our children.

Chapter 12

Holding a balance

The fundamental factors in the educative process are an immature undeveloped being; and certain aims, meanings, values incarnate in the matured experience of the adult. The educative process is the due interaction of these forces. . . .

John Dewey

How does this picture of English compare with what is already happening? Some readers will no doubt be saying that what I have described is what they do and what they see others doing. This may very well be true. It is also true that many teachers do not teach in this way and that those who do are not sustained by any coherent theory. Rather they have to rely on their own enthusiasms and partial support from diverse places. Teachers who try to create a reciprocal, balanced kind of teaching have found themselves cast in the role of reactionary because they are stressing an omission, rather than merely welcoming a new development. They have often believed indeed that they *are* reactionary and have become entrenched in a stubborn stance.

For example if using the framework of *themes* in English means that literature is ransacked and castrated, the teacher is right to resist, yet the easiest step is to reject themes. True, there is danger in the use of a 'theme' but it is possible to collect poems and short stories together that do deal with an important aspect of human experience and to plan all the English work around an exploration of that aspect without doing violence to the poems and stories. Themework needs to be more carefully thought out; 'we need in all thematic teaching to exercise vigilance against the abuse and limitation of the arts.'[151] Themework should be regarded as *one* of our ways of organizing work. In all of them the particular strengths of each kind of work must be recognized.

Resource-based learning, or individualized learning, have their possibilities, too, with that same proviso. (Again, it is literature that is often the main casualty, unless it has a very supportive framework.) There is no need for an either/or choice – there ought to be some work based on reading, some on themes; some class activities, some in groups, some individually undertaken; some teacher-led, some pupil-centred.

If the theory of English teaching were complete it might prevent this wasteful kind of polarization. It would also perhaps temper excessive, partial, claims and the dominance of what is only one aspect of English. No advocates of literature or language have ever demanded the *exclusion* of the other, yet amidst the acerbic claims and counter-claims, it has been difficult for the English teacher to maintain balance. There have been no loud voices in English teaching advocating either complete withdrawal of the teacher or the total subjection of children to the authority of the teacher. Yet what for the teacher is the balance between holding off from the pupil, giving room, and pressing on, insisting, demanding, coercing?

The kind of approach to English that I am pressing attempts to hold in balance a number of countervailing demands.

The pupil must have room to develop personal responses, make choices, including mistakes, take responsibility for his own learning.

The teacher must insist on the qualities of respect, control and attentiveness. Learning must be protected.

Learning is a personal matter; all knowing is that of the knower.

Learning is a public matter involving an accession to what is already known and the adoption of public criteria. Originality comes from knowing and understanding, not from ignorance.

English must recognize the incremental growth of language, its interactive nature, between reading, writing, speaking, listening.

English must work to recognize and promote the special contribution of each of the modes.

Literature plays an essential role in English and in language development.

Literature and reading cannot do any job at all without talk and listening and it is unlikely to do its best work without writing. Literature feeds talk and writing. Literature feeds on talk and writing.

English teaching must relate to the kind of adult life it values; it must therefore involve at times a critical stance to aspects of adult and children's life that hinder this.

The English teacher has to respect what is best in the child and be patient with what is not so good.

The teacher must be prepared to be impatient, coercive where the pupil's welfare and learning are at stake.

Learning English requires respect for and understanding of what has been achieved.

Learning English requires a growing ability to criticize fairly, but if need be adversely, what is offered as achievement.

English must relate to the rest of learning (though that does not mean accepting *all* that goes on in school as learning. One of the problems of the language across the curriculum movement is that it accepts the content of what is learned too readily and attends to the method).

English must concentrate on those areas of experience and language which are its own and so important. The recent publication *Curriculum 11–16* by the D.E.S. makes a distinction between the concerns of the subject English and the wider role of language and learning in the rest of the school, in which the English teacher is *properly* interested, and has, since the publication of the Bullock Report, spent such a gruelling amount of time with.

Integration likewise is something to work towards, but with safe-guards, for the dangers are great of losing sight of what English uniquely offers. It is for what it can *contribute* to other areas that English might join together in integrated work, as well as what we might gain; we contribute nothing if we are not clear what we are doing. We can make connections with art, music, humanities, biology, and we can support the concern with language in schools. This must be done, however, from a clear grasp of the priorities in English. In balancing these elements we must insist on the rightful place of the teacher and the learner (e.g. every teacher must be a learner) on the importance of literature and reading, writing, talking and listening, on the nature of learning as a balance between the person and the culture.

Notes

Introduction

1. *Growth through English*, John Dixon, N.A.T.E., Huddersfield, 1967.

Chapter 1

2. 'Stunting the growth' in *Use of English*, Autumn 1976, Vol. 28/1.
3. *Culture and Environment*, Leavis and Thompson, Chatto, 1933.
4. An alternative way of accounting for the changes at the centre of English teaching would be to analyse the direction taken by N.A.T.E. over the period of its existence.
5. Printed in *A Common Purpose*, ed. J. R. Squire, N.C.T.E., USA, 1966.
6. *Politics*, vii.
7. *Liberal Education in a Technical Society*, Boris Ford, Max Parrish, 1951.
8. *Educational Review*, February 1962.
9. *Use of English*, Summer 1965, Vol. 16/4.
10. *N.A.T.E. Bulletin*, Spring 1965. This experiment has first been reported in the *Educational Review* of February 1962, (Vol. 14, No. 2).
11. 'Library-centred English with Secondary Modern girls', K. Barber, *Use of English*, Summer 1965, Vol. 16/4.
12. *N.A.T.E. Bulletin*, Spring 1965, Vol. 2/1, p. 30.
13. *N.A.T.E. Bulletin*, Summer 1965, Vol. 2/2, p. 40.
14. *Democracy in America*, De Tocqueville, The World's Classics, p. 334.
15. *Spoken English* was published by the University of Birmingham, February 1965.
16. *N.A.T.E. Bulletin*, Spring 1965, Vol. 2/1, p. 25.
17. *Philosophy in a New Key*, Susanne Langer, Harvard, 1942, p. 126.
18. Study Group Paper No. 3, p. 3, *Dartmouth Seminar Papers*, N.C.T.E., 1969. The *Papers* are not paginated serially thoughout.
19. *Rationalism in Politics*, M. Oakeshott, London, 1962.
20. *Democracy in Education*, John Dewey, New York, 1916.
21. 'Education of the teacher of English' *Use of English*, Winter 1966, Vol. 18/2.
22. *English for Maturity*, David Holbrook, C.U.P., 1961, p. 9.
23. 'Creativity in the English programme', p. 3, *Dartmouth Seminar Papers*, N.C.T.E., 1969.
24. *The Disappearing Dais*, Frank Whitehead, Chatto, 1966, p. 18.
25. 'What is "continuity" in English teaching?' *Dartmouth Seminar Papers*, N.C.T.E., 1969.
26. 'Linguistic relevance' *Use of English*, Spring 1965, Vol. 16/3, p. 227. Alan Davies was a member of the 'Oracy' Project.
27. 'Training English teachers in a university Department of Education' *N.A.T.E. Bulletin*, Autumn 1965, Vol. 2/3, p. 5.
28. 'Teaching poetry' *N.A.T.E. Bulletin*, Spring 1966, Vol. 3/1, p. 34.

Chapter 2

29. Albert Markward, Foreword to *Growth through English*, N.A.T.E, Huddersfield, 1967.
30. *The Uses of English*, H. J. Muller, New York, 1967.
31. *Growth through English*, Preface to Second Edition.

135

32. 'Anglo-American exchanges' *Use of English*, Spring 1967, Vol. 18/3.
33. *Growth through English*, p. xi.
34. *Dartmouth Seminar Papers*, N.C.T.E., 1969.
35. This comment is doubly interesting: it suggested an *explicit* role for the centre, unlike most other uses of the term; and it pointed in a timely way to the danger of disintegration by expansion.
36. *Growth through English*, p. 5.
37. Response to 'What is English?', *Dartmouth Seminar Papers*, N.C.T.E., 1969.
38. *The Disappearing Dais*, p. 13.
39. *Growth through English*, p. 1.
40. *The School and the Curriculum*, Chicago, 1902, p. 73.
41. 'Raids on the inarticulate', D. W. Harding, *Use of English*, Winter 1967, Vol. 19/2.
42. 'Response to literature', Study Group Paper No. 5, p. 1, *Dartmouth Seminar Papers*, N.C.T.E., 1969.
43. *The Uses of English*, p. 77.
44. 'Cultural heritage' ('Response to Literature' Appendix III) p. 2, *Dartmouth Seminar Papers*, N.C.T.E., 1969.
45. Not quite, as I have shown.
46. 'The teaching of English', p. 2 (Working Party IV), *Dartmouth Seminar Papers*, N.C.T.E., 1969.
47. 'What is continuity in English?', p. 6, *Dartmouth Seminar Papers*, N.C.T.E., 1969.

Chapter 3
48. *Growth through English*, p. 33.
49. *Directions in the Teaching of English*, ed. Thompson, Cambridge, 1969, p. 25.
50. *Topics in English*, G. Summerfield, Batsford, 1965.
51. *Team Teaching and the Teaching of English*, A. Adams, Pergamon, 1970.
52. A bizarre example in a Sheffield school in the early seventies was the use of *Kestrel for a Knave* in several pieces, months apart, in the themes of Predators, Violence, Family Life, Loneliness, etc.
53. 'Using children's novels as a starting-point', J. Marder, *Use of English*, Spring 1969, Vol. 20/3.
54. *The Humanities Jungle*, A. Adams, Ward Lock, 1976.
55. 'English and humanities', D. Lindley, *Use of English*, Spring 1973, Vol. 24/3.
56. 'Literature in use', B. Hollingworth, *Use of English*, Spring 1973, Vol. 24/3.

Chapter 4
57. See Chapter 1.
58. M. K. Halliday, Preface to *The Relevance of Linguistics to the English Teacher*, P. S. Doughty, Longman, 1968.
59. The chapter by Harold Rosen for *Talking and Writing*, 'The Language of Textbooks', was in fact written for the Dartmouth Seminar – the book can be seen as a development of some of the directions in thinking shown there.
60. 'Linguistics and relevance', N. Postman, *Use of English*, 1968, Vol. 20/1.
61. 'Modern views of English language', W. Mittins, *English in Education*, Spring 1969, Vol. 3/1. This was a reprint of an article originally published in *Aspects of Education* (Hull, 1966) but that the article was still thought to be alive indicates something of the state of thinking.
62. Response to 'What is English?', p. 3, *Dartmouth Seminar Papers*, N.C.T.E., 1969.
63. 'Language', in *Directions in the Teaching of English*, ed. Thompson, C.U.P., 1969.
64. Inglis' remarks were subsequently published in *English in Education*, 1971, Vol. 5/2, as 'How to do things with words: a critique of language studies'.
65. 'Pupils also use language to live', P. Doughty, *English in Education*, Spring 1972, Vol. 6/1.
66. '*Language in use* – another viewpoint', D. Salter, *English in Education*, Spring 1973, Vol. 7/1.

67.   'Language and experience', L. Stratta, *English in Education*, Autumn 1972, Vol. 6/3.
68.   *A Language for Life* (Bullock Report), H.M.S.O., 1975.

Chapter 5
69.   *New Movements in the Study and Teaching of English*, ed. N. Bagnall, Temple Smith, 1973.
70.   'Response to literature', p. 9, *Dartmouth Seminar Papers*, N.C.T.E., 1969.
71.   'The role of the onlooker', D. W. Harding, *Scrutiny* 1937, Vol. 6/3, pp. 247–258.
72.   *Talking and Writing*, ed. J. Britton, Methuen, 1967.
73.   'Response to literature', p. 11, *Dartmouth Seminar Papers*, N.C.T.E., 1969.
74.   *Language and Learning*, J. Britton, Allen Lane, 1970, p. 7.
75.   See above p. 16.
76.   See Chapter 4, p. 50.
77.   See *From Communication to Curriculum*, D. Barnes, Penguin, 1976.
78.   'How to do things with words', F. Inglis, *English in Education*, Summer 1971, Vol. 5/2. As far as I can discover, Britton, unlike Peter Doughty, never replied to the criticisms, nor were they taken up to any degree elsewhere, yet they seem substantive enough to be debated.
79.   See Note 69 above, p. 27.

Chapter 6
80.   'One road or many?' *Dartmouth Seminar Papers*, N.C.T.E., 1969.
81.   *Social Class and Educational Opportunities*, A. H. Halsey and J. Floud, Heinemann, 1957.
82.   *The Home and the School*, J. W. B. Douglas, MacGibbon and Kee, 1964.
83.   *Education and the Working Class*, B. Jackson and B. Marsden, Routledge, 1962.
84.   *Half our Future* (Newsom Report), H.M.S.O., 1963.
85.   *Social Class, Language and Education*, D. Lawton, Routledge, 1968.
86.   *Educational Priority*, Vol. 1, A. H. Halsey, H.M.S.O., 1970, p. 5.
87.   *Team Teaching and the Teaching of English*, A. Adams, Pergamon, 1970, p. 3.
88.   'Going comprehensive', E. Jones, *Use of English*, Autumn 1971, Vol. 22/3.
89.   Editorial, A. Adams, *English in Education*, Autumn 1970, Vol. 4/3.
90.   See Note 88 above.
91.   'It's later than you think', F. Flower, *English in Education*, Summer 1967, Vol. 1/2.
92.   'You're no better'n us', M. Cullup, *Use of English*, Summer 1967, Vol. 18/4.
93.   Schools Council Working Paper II.
94.   'Z-Cars and the teacher', M. Marland, *Use of English*, Spring 1967, Vol. 18/3.
95.   'Existentialism writ small', B. Hollingworth, *Use of English*, Winter 1969, Vol. 21/2.
96.   'The Bernstein of "Open Schools: Open Society"', *New Society*, 14 September, 1967.
97.   'Karl Popper and the English teacher', B. Hollingworth, *Use of English*, Spring 1974, Vol. 25/3.
98.   This macrocosm of the political nature of English studies was reflected in the small world of a school bookshop, in an article by Roger Lewis: 'Here, in the organization of a bookshop, is an excellent opportunity to allow the children to come through to a democratic awareness'.
      'The school bookshop: an experiment in democratic control.' *Use of English*, Vol. 21/2, 1969.
99.   'Literature in use', B. Hollingworth, *Use of English*, Summer 1973, Vol. 24/3.
100. 'New approaches – the novel', S. Bolt, *English in Education*, Summer 1969, Vol. 3/2.
101. *The Teaching of English in Schools 1900–1970*, D. Shayer, Routledge, 1972.

Chapter 7
102. 'Guidance of extensive reading at the top end of the Secondary Modern School', J. D. Carsley, *Educational Review*, 1953.
103. 'Literature broadly conceived', F. S. Whitehead, *N.A.T.E. Bulletin*, Summer 1966, Vol. 3/2.

104. 'Literature in the Secondary School', M. Tucker, *N.A.T.E. Bulletin*, Summer 1966, Vol. 3/2.
105. *Patterns of Language*, L. Stratta, J. Dixon and A. Wilkinson, Heinemann, 1973.
106. 'Enjoying reading', B. Hankins, *Use of English*, Summer 1968, Vol. 19/4.
107. 'Readers or literature?', M. Tucker, *Use of English*, Spring 1968, Vol. 19/3.
108. 'Enjoying reading', J. M. Batten, *Use of English*, Summer 1969, Vol. 20/4.
109. 'Popular reading or literature?', O. Gaggs, *Use of English*, Winter 1969, Vol. 21/2.
110. 'S.F. in the classroom', R. Sampson, *English in Education*, Summer 1972, Vol. 6/2.
111. 'Contemporary fiction in the Secondary School', J. Powell, *Use of English*, Spring 1975, Vol. 26/3.
112. 'Possible future co-operative activities', p. 2, *Dartmouth Seminar Papers*, N.C.T.E., 1969.
113. Frank Whitehead in *Reading Together*, K. Calthrop, Heinemann, 1971, p. iii.
114. *Children and their Books*, F. S. Whitehead *et al*, Macmillan, 1977.
115. 'The next stage', F. S. Whitehead, *English in Education*, Summer 1967, Vol. 1/2.
116. *The Right Response*, S. F. Bolt, Hutchinson, 1966.
117. 'Teaching English on the border-line', S. F. Bolt, *English in Education*, Summer 1967, Vol. 1/2.
118. *Teaching Fiction in Schools*, S. F. Bolt and R. Gard, Hutchinson, 1970.
119. 'Report from a strange research project', F. Inglis, *Use of English*, Spring 1967, Vol. 18/3.
120. *The Englishness of English Teaching*, F. Inglis, Longman, 1969.
121. 'English in a college of education', J. R. Osgerby, *Use of English*, Summer 1970, Vol. 21/4.
122. 'The precious life-blood', A. C. Capey, *Use of English*, Winter 1970, Vol. 22/2.

Chapter 8
123. 'Growth through English', J. A. M. Baldwin, *Use of English*, Autumn 1973, Vol. 25/1.
124. 'A rage for disorder', Albert Kitzhaber, *Use of English*, Winter 1973, Vol. 25/3.
125. 'Stunting the growth', F. S. Whitehead, *Use of English*, Autumn 1976, Vol. 28/1.
126. 'What's the use, indeed?', F. S. Whitehead, *Use of English*, Spring 1978, Vol. 29/2.
127. 'Going back inside', Pat D'Arcy, *Times Educational Supplement*, 29.1.77.
128. See 'A different form' by Geraldine Murray, as an example of just that belief, *English in Education*, Autumn 1978, Vol. 12/1.
129. *Use of English*, Autumn 1978, Vol. 30/1, pp. 52–55.

Chapter 9
130. *A Language for Life*, H.M.S.O., 1975, p. xxxv.
131. *English for Diversity*, Peter Abbs, Heinemann, 1969, p. 52.
132. I have taken the term from Lawrence, who uses it in *Studies in Classic American Literature*, Thomas Seltzer Inc, U.S.A., 1923. The force that Lawrence was pointing to is in his comment, 'Art-speech is the only truth. An artist is usually a damned liar, but his art, if it be art, will tell you the truth of his day.' I have adapted, somewhat extended, the notion, from what Lawrence had in mind, while, I hope, retaining the central point.
133. *Phoenix*, D. H. Lawrence, London, 1936, p. 527.
134. *Survival of English*, I. Robinson, C.U.P., 1973.
135. 'Where will all the English go?', Gordon Mason, *Times Educational Supplement*, 2 June 1978.

Chapter 10
136. This has been developed by Douglas Barnes into a division of teaching styles into either *transmission* or *interpretation* – the latter involves the learner in making the meaning his own. See *From Communication to Curriculum*, D. Barnes, Penguin, 1976.

137. See the writings of G. H. Bantock, R. S. Peters, Michael Oakeshott. They all three urge the *reciprocal* nature of education between child and culture, yet are regarded as reactionary by the enlightened English teacher.
138. *Personal Knowledge*, Michael Polanyi, Routledge, 1958. All the quotations ascribed to Polanyi are taken from this book.

Chapter 11
139. *Experience into Words*, D. W. Harding, Chatto, 1963, p. 9.
140. *Children and their Books*, F. S. Whitehead and others, Macmillan, 1977.
141. *Understanding Reading*, Frank Smith, Holt, Reinhart, Winston, 1971, p. 53.
142. *What the Neighbours Did*, P. Pearce, Puffin, 1977.
143. *Reading Development and Extension*, C. Walker, Ward Lock, 1974.
144. *Spoken English*, ed. A. Wilkinson, Birmingham University Press, 1965, p. 11.
145. 'Teaching English', Roger Harcourt, *Use of English*, Summer 1973, Vol. 24/1.
146. *English for Maturity*, David Holbrook, C.U.P., 1961.
147. *Teaching English*, J. H. Walsh, Heinemann, 1965.
148. 'When in doubt, write a poem', R. Protherough, *English in Education*, Spring 1978, Vol. 12/1, pp. 9–21.
149. *English for Diversity*, Peter Abbs, Heinemann, 1969.
150. *Discrimination and Popular Culture*, ed. D. Thompson, Heinemann, 1973.

Chapter 12
151. *Humanities Jungle*, A. Adams, Ward Lock, 1976, p. 54.

Bibliography

This has been arranged in chronological order so that anyone interested can follow the evolution of ideas.

NB. For simplicity, the journal *Use of English* is referred to throughout by its initials (*U.E.*), and *English in Education* as *E.E.*

Before 1965
Aristotle, *Politics*.
De Toqueville, *Democracy in America*.
Dewey, John, *The School and the Curriculum*, Univ. of Chicago, 1902; *The School and Society*, Univ. of Chicago, 1910; *Democracy in Education*, Macmillan, New York, 1916.
Lawrence, D. H., *Studies in Classic American Literature*, Thomas Seltzer Inc, USA, 1923; 'Education of the people', in *Phoenix*, Heinemann, 1936; 'Morality and the novel', *Calendar of Modern Letters*, 1925 (printed in *Phoenix*).
Harding, D. W., 'Role of the onlooker', *Scrutiny*, Vol. 6/3, 1937.
National Society for the Study of Education, *The Teaching of Reading – 36th Year Book*, National Society for the Study of Education, Bloomington, USA, 1937.
Langer, S. K., *Philosophy in a New Key*, Harvard, 1942.
Carsley, J. D., 'Guidance of extensive reading', *Educ. Review*, 1953.
Halsey, A. H. (and J. Floud), *Social Class and Educational Opportunities*, Heinemann, 1957.
Polanyi, M., *Personal Knowledge*, Routledge, 1958.
Holbrook, D., *English for Maturity*, C.U.P., 1961.
Jackson, B. (and B. Marsden), *Education and the Working Class*, Routledge, 1962.
Jackson, B. (and D. Thompson) (eds), *English in Education*, Chatto, 1962.
Oakeshott, M., *Rationalism in Politics*, Methuen, 1962.
Harding, D. W., *Experience into Words*, Chatto, 1963.
Newsom, Sir John, *Half our Future* (Newsom Report), H.M.S.O., 1963.
Douglas, J. W. B., *The Home and the School*, MacGibbon, 1964.
Clegg, Sir Alec (ed), *The Excitement of Writing*, Chatto, 1964.

1965
Barber. K., 'Library-centred English with Secondary Modern girls', *U.E.*, Summer, Vol. 16/4.
Brewer, D., 'The School of English and English in Schools', *N.A.T.E. Bulletin*, Autumn, Vol. 2/3.
Britton, J., 'Speech in the school', *N.A.T.E. Bulletin*, Summer, Vol. 2/2.
Davies, A., 'Linguistic Relevance', *U.E.*, Spring, Vol. 16/3.
Druce, R., *Eye of Innocence*, Brockhampton.
Heath, W. G., 'Library-centred English', *N.A.T.E. Bulletin*, Spring, Vol. 2/1.
Hipkin, J., 'Report on a reading scheme', *U.E.*, Summer, Vol. 16/4.
Jackson, B., *English versus Examinations*, Chatto.
Martin, N., 'Training English Teachers in a University Department of Education', *N.A.T.E. Bulletin*, Vol. 2/3.
McElroy, 'Books for the over-fourteens', *U.E.*, Autumn, Vol. 17/1.
N.A.T.E., 'Some aspects of oracy', *N.A.T.E. Bulletin*, Summer, Vol. 2/2.
Squires, J. C. (ed), *A Common Purpose*, N.C.T.E., USA.

Summerfield, G., *Topics in English*, Batsford.
Walsh, J. H., *Teaching English*, Heinemann.
Whitehead, F. S., 'Reading and literature in the examining of English', *U.E.*, Summer, Vol. 16/4.
Wilkinson, A., *Spoken English*, Birmingham University Press.

1966
Bolt, S. F., *The Right Response*, Hutchinson; 'Unqualified readers', *U.E.*, Spring, Vol. 17/3.
Dixon, J., 'Literature in Higher Education', *N.A.T.E. Bulletin*, Summer, Vol. 3/2.
Doughty, P., 'Teaching poetry', *N.A.T.E. Bulletin*, Spring, Vol. 3/1.
Flower, F., *Language and Education*, Longman.
Harris, R., 'Education of the teacher of English', *U.E.*, Winter, Vol. 18/2.
Thompson, D., 'What is literature?', *N.A.T.E Bulletin*, Summer, Vol. 3/2.
Tucker, M., 'Literature in the Secondary School', *N.A.T.E. Bulletin*, Summer, Vol. 3/2.
Whitehead, F. S., 'Literature broadly conceived', *N.A.T.E. Bulletin*, Summer, Vol. 3/2; *The Disappearing Dais*, Chatto.

1967
Bolt, S. F., 'Teaching English on the border line', *E.E.*, Summer, Vol. 1/2.
Britton, J. (ed), *Talking and Writing*, Methuen.
Butts, D., 'A trifle temperamental (Literature and CSE)', *U.E.*, Summer, Vol. 18/4.
Creber, J. W. P., *Sense and Sensitivity*, U.L.P; 'Current trends', *E.E.*, Spring, Vol. 1/1.
Cullup, M., 'You're no better'n us', *U.E.*, Summer, Vol. 18/4.
Dixon, J., *Growth through English*, N.A.T.E., Huddersfield.
Flower, F., 'It's later than you think', *E.E.*, Summer, Vol. 1/2.
Harding, D. W., 'Considered experience', *E.E.*, Summer, Vol. 18/4; 'Raids on the inarticulate', *U.E.*, Winter, Vol. 19/2.
Inglis, F., 'Report from a strange research project', *U.E.*, Spring, Vol. 18/3.
Marland, M., 'Z-Cars and the teacher', *U.E.*, Spring, Vol. 18/3.
Muller, H. J., *The Uses of English*, Holt, Rinehart, Winston.
Thompson, D., 'Anglo-American exchanges', *U.E.*, Spring, Vol. 18/3.
Whitehead, F. S., 'The next stage', *E.E.*, Summer, Vol. 1/2.
Wilson, R., 'Linguistics and standards', *U.E.*, Spring, Vol. 18/2.

1968
Doughty, P. S., *The Relevance of Linguistics to the English Teacher*, Longman; *Linguistics and the Teaching of English*, Longman.
Hankins, B., 'Enjoying reading', *U.E.*, Summer, Vol. 19/4.
Lawton, D., *Social Class, Language and Education*, Routledge.
Lewis, E. G., 'Postscript to Dartmouth – or poles apart?', *College English*, No. 29.
Postman, N., 'Linguistics and relevance', *U.E.*, Vol. 20/1.
Squire, J. C., 'International perspective on the teaching of English', *College English*, No. 29.
Tucker, M., 'Readers or literature?', *U.E.*, Spring, Vol. 19/3.

1969
N.C.T.E., *Dartmouth Seminar Papers*, N.C.T.E., USA.
Abbs, P., *English for Diversity*, Heinemann.
Adams, A., 'Team teaching and the English teacher', *U.E.*, Autumn, Vol. 21/1.
Barnes, D. et al, *Language Learner and the School*, Penguin.
Batten, J. M., 'Enjoying reading', *U.E.*, Summer, Vol. 20/4.
Bolt, S., 'New approaches – the novel', *E.E.*, Summer, Vol. 3/2.
Dixon, J., 'A new tradition in English teaching', *E.E.*, Summer, Vol. 3/2; 'Conference Report – Dartmouth Seminar', *Harvard Educ. Review*, No. 39.
Gaggs, O., 'Popular reading or literature?', *U.E.*, Winter, Vol. 21/2.

Hollingsworth, B., 'Existentialism writ small', *U.E.*, Winter, Vol. 21/2.
Inglis, F., *Englishness of English Teaching*, Longman.
Lewis, R., 'The school bookshop', *U.E.*, Winter, Vol. 21/2.
Marder, J., 'Using children's novels as starting-points', *U.E.*, Spring, Vol. 20/3.
Mittins, W., 'Modern views of English language', *E.E.*, Spring, Vol. 3/1.
Thompson, D. (ed), *Directions in Teaching of English*, C.U.P.

1970
Adams, A., *Team Teaching and the Teaching of English*, Pergamon; Editorial, *E.E.*, Autumn, Vol. 4/3.
Bolt, S. (with Gard, R.), *Teaching Fiction in Schools*, Hutchinson.
Britton, J. N., 'Their language and our teaching', *E.E.*, Summer, Vol. 4/2; *Language and Learning*, Allen Lane.
Capey, A., 'The precious life-blood', *U.E.*, Winter, Vol. 22/2.
Creber, P. W., 'An imaginative/critical model for secondary schools', *E.E.*, Summer, Vol. 4/2.
Halsey, A. H., *Educational Priority*, Vol. 1, H.M.S.O.
Hourd, M., 'English and continuity', *E.E.*, Summer, Vol. 4/2.
Jones, E., 'The language of failure', *E.E.*, Autumn, Vol. 4/3.
Osgerby, J. R., 'English in a college of education', *U.E.*, Summer, Vol. 21/4.
Owens, G. (ed), *Practice of English Teaching*, Blackie.
Robertson, G., 'Looking for continuity', *E.E.*, Summer, Vol. 4/2.
Whitehead, F. S., 'Continuity in English teaching', *U.E.*, Autumn, Vol. 22/1.
Wilkinson, E., 'Coherence in practice', *E.E.*, Summer, Vol. 4/2.

1971
Barnes, D., 'Classroom contexts for language learning', *Educ. Review*, No. 23; 'Group talk and literary response', *E.E.*, Autumn, Vol. 5/3.
Blackie, P., 'Asking questions (in teaching literature)', *E.E.*, Autumn, Vol. 5/3.
Britton, J., 'York International Conference 1971', *E.E.*, Spring, Vol. 6/1; 'Learning from each other', *Times Educ. Supplement*, 26 November; 'Role of fantasy', *E.E.*, Autumn, Vol. 5/3.
Calthrop, K., *Reading Together: the use of the class reader*, Heinemann.
Doughty, P., *Language in Use*, Arnold.
Harding, D. W., 'The bond with the author', *U.E.*, Summer, Vol. 22/4.
Inglis, F., 'How to do things with words', *E.E.*, Summer, Vol. 5/2.
Jones, R., 'Going comprehensive', *U.E.*, Autumn, Vol. 22/3.
Miller, J. E., 'What happened at Dartmouth?', *U.E.*, Winter, Vol. 23/2.
Rosenblatt, L., 'Pattern and process', *U.E.*, Spring, Vol. 22/3.
Sharp, D., 'Structure – a plea for synthesis', *U.E.*, Winter, Vol. 23/2.
Sinclair, J., 'The integration of language and literature', *Educ. Review*, No. 23.
Smith. F., *Understanding Reading*, Holt, Rinehart, USA.
Summerfield, G. (ed), *English in Practice*, C.U.P.

1972
Ashwin, J., 'Themes *v.* literature', *U.E.*, Winter, Vol. 23/2.
Creber, J. W. P., *Lost for Words*, Penguin.
Doughty, P., 'Pupils also use language to live', *E.E.*, Spring, Vol. 6/1.
Douglas, W. W., 'An American view of the failure of curriculum reform', *E.E.*, Summer, Vol. 6/2.
Hollindale, P., 'Why have things gone wrong?', *U.E.*, Summer, Vol. 23/4.
Sampson, R., 'S.F. in the classroom', *E.E.*, Summer, Vol. 6/2.
Shayer, D., *Teaching of English in Schools 1900–1970*, Routledge.
Smith, L. E. W., *Towards a New English Curriculum*, Dent.
Squire, J. R., 'Freedom and constraint', *E.E.*, Spring, Vol. 6/1.
Stratta, L., 'English and sociology in the secondary school', *Journal of Curric. Studies*, No. 4; 'Language and experience', *E.E.*, Autumn, Vol. 6/3.

1973
Bagnall, N. (ed), *New Movements in the Study and Teaching of English*, Temple Smith.
Baldwin, J. A. M., 'Growth through English', *U.E.*, Autumn, Vol. 25/1.
Britton, J., 'Ten years of N.A.T.E.', *E.E.*, Summer, Vol. 7/2.
Harcourt, R., 'Teaching English today', *U.E.*, Summer, Vol. 24/4.
Hardy, B., 'The teaching of literature in the University', *E.E.*, Spring, Vol. 7/1.
Hollingworth, B., 'Literature in use', *U.E.*, Summer, Vol. 24/3.
Kitzhaber, A. R., 'A rage for disorder', *U.E.*, Winter, Vol. 25/2.
Lindley, D., 'English and humanities', *U.E.*, Spring, Vol. 24/3.
Robinson, I., *Survival of English*, C.U.P.
Salter, D., 'Language in use – another viewpoint', *E.E.*, Spring, Vol. 7/1.
Stratta, L. (et. al.), *Patterns of Language*, Heinemann.

1974
Adams, A., *Every English Teacher*, O.U.P.
Britton, J., 'What is "English"?', *Trends in Education*, No. 36.
Burke, S. J. (with C. J. Brumfit), 'Is literature language or language literature?', *E.E.*, Spring, Vol. 8/1.
Dixon, J., *Growth through English* (3rd edition, amended), O.U.P.
Doughty, P., *Language, English and the Curriculum*, Arnold.
Harcourt, R., 'Sharing poems', *U.E.*, Summer, Vol. 25/4.
Hollingworth, B., 'Karl Popper and the English teacher', *U.E.*, Spring, Vol. 25/3.
Kefford, R. E., 'On the relevance of relevance', *U.E.*, Winter, Vol. 26/2.
Mills, R., 'Small group discussion', *E.E.*, Summer, Vol. 8/2.
Protherough, R., 'Changing ideas of literature', *E.E.*, Summer, Vol. 8/2.
Robson, C. B., 'Coalface Blues', *U.E.*, Winter, Vol. 26/2.
Rusk, D., 'The distorting mirror', *U.E.*, Summer, Vol. 25/4.
Thompson, D., 'Poetry in schools', *U.E.*, Winter, Vol. 26/2.
Tunnicliffe, S., 'Turning and turning in the widening gyre', *U.E.*, Summer, Vol. 25/4.
Warlow, A., 'Children and literature', *E.E.*, Autumn, Vol. 8/3.

1975
Aers, L., 'Mind forg'd manacles', *E.E.*, Spring, Vol. 9/1.
Bullock Report, *A Language for Life*, H.M.S.O.
Hand, N., 'Slince, little children, slince', *U.E.*, Summer, Vol. 26/4.
Inglis, F., 'Against proportional representation', *E.E.*, Spring, Vol. 9/1.
Mathieson, M., 'Ideology of English teaching', *Educ. for Teaching*, No. 98; *Preachers of Culture*, Allen and Unwin.
Powell, J., 'Contemporary fiction in the Secondary School', *U.E.*, Spring, Vol. 26/3.
Whitebrook, M., 'The political element in English literature', *E.E.*, Spring, Vol. 9/1.

1976
Adams, A., *The Humanities Jungle*, Ward Lock.
Barnes, D., *From Communication to Curriculum*, Penguin.
Whitehead, F. S., 'Stunting the growth', *U.E.*, Autumn, Vol. 28/1.

1977
D.E.S., *Curriculum 11–16*, H.M.S.O.
D'Arcy, 'Going back inside', *T.E.S.*, 8 January.
Whitehead, F. S. and others, *Children and their Books*, Macmillan.

1978
Dixon, J., 'Kinds of writing', *U.E.*, Autumn, Vol. 30/1.
Murray, G., 'A different form', *E.E.*, Autumn, Vol. 12/3.
Protherough, R., 'When in doubt, write a poem', *E.E.*, Spring, Vol. 12/1.
Whitehead, F. S., 'What's the use, indeed?', *U.E.*, Vol. 29/2.

Index

144